Accessory to Marriage

A Chronicle of Outrageousness from

my Life as a Wedding Photographer

By James D. Walters

©2013 James D. Walters
ISBN-10 1483932397
EAN-13 9781483932392
Library of Congress Control Number: 2013905990
CreateSpace Independent Publishing
Platform North Charleston, South Carolina

For Will and Grace, who patiently put up

with our absence most Saturdays—

and for Meridith, who has always been there.

Table of Contents

Acknowledgments

I am fortunate to have the interest and enthusiasm of a wonderful group of friends and colleagues who also happen to be exceptional wedding and event professionals. This community has been outstanding in its encouragement, inspiration, and support of this book.

Many of you have expressed desire to write your stories down for others to enjoy. If you do, I look forward to giving you the support that you have so generously given to me and to this project.

Jason Huggins—When I first showed you this manuscript years ago, you read it and said, "Show me what's happening in each story" rather than just telling the story. That was great advice.

Meridith—Upon showing you this set of stories years ago, you said, "develop them more. Bring the reader into the stories." I groaned and told you that would be a lot of work. It was a lot more work than I imagined, but I think it will be worth it. Thanks for pushing me.

Martha Manning—You were a sounding board and an encourager long before this book was a thing.

Robin Lin—My insightful and intuitive friend. Thank you for saving me from my literary self.

Laura Petersen—Every team needs a cheerleader and advocate and you are one of the best. Thank you for bringing your energy to this experience.

Beth Jarvah—You spread your sunshine every time you're around. Thanks for bringing your positivity.

Despina Curtis and the Viniotis Family—Thank you for believing in this. You and your family are very special to Meridith and me. Thank you also for helping to keep us grounded and reminding us why we do what we do.

Joe Bunn—It's been a wild dozen years that we've worked together so far. I'd say, "Here's to a dozen more," but I've discovered that wedding seasons are kind of like dog years in the way they make us age. If that's the case, a dozen years from now we will feel like we're in our late nineties!

Robin Grathwol— You are a powerful example of creativity, persistence and hard work. I have learned so much from you.

I'd like to extend a special thanks to a group of people who made this book possible as the generous and enthusiastic backers of the KickStarter campaign that funded the editing, graphic design, and first print run of this book. Without you this book would still be a file on my computer and a fun idea that might happen someday. Because of your involvement, this book is for real now, and I hope it will spread laughter and not too many paper cuts to others for years to come.

Kevin DeHimer	Eva Rose Kennedy
Jennifer LeRay	Robyn Mangrum
Jessica Norwood	Steve Stowe
Cara Galati	Megan Gillikin
Terry Elvers	Mary Anne Yow Odom
Elizabeth Myers	Sarah Litty

Amanda Benton

Joe Payne

Neil Boyd

James Auerbach

Katie Dunn

Adelaide Stallings

Lisa Kelly

Kevin Milz

Brian McGuire

Michelle McMurray

Shelley Cooper-White

Despina Curtis

Chris & Toni Wheaton

Randy Bennett

Donna Parks

Stacy Sibbach

Jenny Zsuppan

Margaret Smith

Rebecca Ferguson

Cheree Brown

Angie Wright

Marissa Swart

Eli J Lewis

Cyndie Hatcher

Jeff Poole

Jenn Aan

Ashley Vacha

John Hayes

Amanda Scott

Stacy Borelli

Erin McLean

Teresa Porter

Melissa Windley

Beth Jarvah

Rick Bryda

Cara Shirley

Danielle Massey

Ryan Pflumm

Kristy

Tim Sayer

Michael Mcatee

William Roeder

Daniel Chachakis

Dana Mcatee

Allen Smith

Kristen Klett

Clarissa Elena

Jonathan Johnson

Jessica Siciliano

Shelly Keeter

Preface

This wasn't supposed to happen. Not to me at least. When I went to college to pursue my dream of a career behind a camera, I never imagined that it would lead me to weddings. In photography school, the perception was that you became a wedding photographer if you couldn't handle the big stuff, like ad campaigns or assignments in exotic places for a newspaper or magazine. That was the kind of work you dreamed about. Quick—name a photographer whose work you could see in a major museum. You probably blurted out Lebovitz, Adams, Avedon, or Bresson (if you took an art class in college). Can you think of any wedding photographers on that level? I didn't think so. My impression of weddings back then put them in the same category with photographing crying babies and cat calendars. It just didn't seem cool when you're twenty years old and full of yourself.

As my career unfolded, I did a lot of the things I dreamed about, like working in interesting locations, shooting for big ad campaigns, and working with well-known artists and sports figures. As a commercial and advertising photographer for more than a decade, I collaborated with incredibly talented art directors, interior designers, graphic artists, prop stylists, makeup artists, models, set builders, assistants, and clients. Each person I met added to my experience by pushing me to be more creative and produce excellence.

Then I got burned out.

While each day in the studio was different and challenging, photographing ads for the next hot product or even lingerie is not always inspiring. In fact, most of the creative opportunities lie in problem solving. Usually an art director would bring me a sketch of an idea the client had already signed off on. My job was to take it from concept to photograph with little room for creative interpretation.

For the first decade of my career, I was excited just to learn, work with talented people, and create interesting and well-executed images. After ten years I thought about the fact that once the ad had run or the magazine was off the shelf, the images that I along with an extensive team of creative people poured ourselves into were no longer relevant, except to us in our portfolios. I had been consumed with learning and perfecting my craft. Every photo shoot was an opportunity to learn more, but after ten years, the learning wasn't happening as often. I needed to move on, but I had no idea what moving on would involve.

Out of nowhere, I got a call from Tom Edwards. I had met Tom nearly a decade earlier when I was in photo school. He specialized in weddings and contacted the school looking for an assistant. Being nineteen years old with no weekend plans, I jumped at the chance to gain some real world experience. I assisted him on Saturdays holding the light meter, moving lights, changing film (yes film, it was a thing), and in general just trying to be helpful. As an introverted artistic type, it could be said that my people skills were just a notch above deplorable. So I really wanted to see how Tom worked with his subjects. Since he was paying my gas money for each gig, I had no reason not to. I learned a lot from him back then, but I was still quite certain that I would never shoot a wedding myself. Once I began my final year of school and entered the commercial photography program, I parted ways with Tom to concentrate on my studies.

A few months before he called, I had run into Tom in a retouching class at a photo convention. It was the first time I'd talked to him in years, and now he was calling to ask if I wanted to shoot weddings for his studio.

I thought for a minute and said, "Nope, that's just not my thing."

My weekends were filled shooting composite cards for modeling agencies, and I loved it. A few months passed, and I received another call. This time Tom explained that his associate photographer had bailed on him to move to Atlanta. He asked if I could help him out with two weddings. Anyone who knows me knows that I will jump in to help in times of crisis. So I said, "Sure, why not? Just two jobs, should be interesting."

What followed was two and a half years of shooting weddings for Tom's studio, a major paradigm shift, and new appreciation for photography itself. After the first few weddings, I looked forward to the rush of knowing that I was photographing something important for the families. I was now the one calling all of the creative shots in an unpredictable and mostly uncontrollable situation where I couldn't spend all day getting things perfect. It turned out to be just the challenge that I needed to keep me interested in my chosen career.

Another great thing happened during that period of time. People's acceptance of less formal wedding photography was emerging, and our couples loved the work we were delivering to them. They liked that the images looked more modern than when their sister got married, and they commented often that the photos looked like they should be in a magazine.

It was nice to hear the compliments. But I wasn't setting the world on fire or doing anything that had never been attempted. I was simply trying to create photos that looked natural and showed the beauty of the moment. I was excited and a little surprised that the brides were so receptive to my work.

In the past, it was standard procedure to photograph the family lined up around the bride and groom and smiling pleasantly. We still do a lot of that. But I swore off the stuff that doesn't really happen naturally, like ring hands on the Bible, or groomsmen picking up the bride. Or that photo you've seen where the bridesmaids place their bouquets in a circle and the bride peeks through, as if she's some sort of Rose Parade float.

I chose to photograph things in a less contrived way, one in which you would look at the image and say to yourself, "Yeah, I can see that happening." It was important for me to create photos that those people would still want to look at in twenty years—relaxed, beautiful, and real. People ate it up.

At that point in my career, I was finally feeling in control creatively. It almost began to feel cool to shoot weddings. Well, almost. I say that because in that time of transition I was still shooting for commercial clients and was scared to let it slip that I had anything to do with weddings. I feared that my commercial clients would have the same perception about wedding photographers that I once did. So I kept my mouth shut. For about three years I lead a double life of commercial clients during the week and weddings on Saturdays. Needless to say, I didn't get much sleep and something had to give.

That's when my wife and I made the decision to do our own thing. I let go of my commercial job, and Meridith and I went full force into weddings. It feels good to know that now when we create photographs for our clients, the images we produce will not have a shelf life. They will be cherished forever —or as long as the couple likes each other. That's a pretty motivating thought. We are providing a personal history for them. So what if sometimes we make it look better than what really happened, or if they look more in love than they actually are? Our clients don't want to look good. They want to look extraordinarily fantabulous (say that three times fast).

At its core, what I do with a wedding is not very different from an advertising project. Instead of trying to sell a product with a photograph, I'm selling an idea. The images created at a wedding showcase the idea that two people are in love and will be happy forever. That everything was beautiful on the wedding day, and everyone was sincere and well behaved. No matter what the day brings, it is expected that we deliver perfection at every event.

Things have changed a lot since photo school. Now it seems that people in general think wedding photographers have the coolest, easiest, best job around. Many are lining up to get into it. I hear all too often from people who have suddenly decided to become photographers, and their main plan of action is to book some weddings so they can practice at getting better. The "fake it till you make it" mentality seems to be the order of the day. I feel sorry for the unsuspecting couples that fall for it. The memories from their wedding day will be impacted, for better or for worse, by the person behind the camera.

We have had the opportunity to be a part of hundreds of wonderful celebrations. Some of our clients have been more entertaining than others and being "backstage" with them during such an important time is truly a privilege. All the same, we've seen some crazy stuff that we just couldn't keep to ourselves. This book is for anyone who has ever had a morbid fascination with wedding-related drama. Mostly though, it's a cautionary tale for those getting married in the future.

Introduction

You know that old cliché about how ignorance is bliss? If it's true, then the pages of this book are filled with in-your-face and up-side-your-head wedded bliss. Most people are interested in what happens behind the scenes in situations like weddings, where emotions run high and those involved are either on the verge of creating something wonderful, or acting out their part of a freak show.

Several hundred weddings ago, my wife Meridith and I noticed that weddings are incubators for the unexpected. Anything can happen. Though most weddings go off without a hitch, the juiciest stories play out behind the scenes. Arguments, tears, jokes, breakdowns, and drama—as wedding photographers, we are there, and we see it all! We are accomplices to our couples on their wedding day, standing close by to observe, document, and help things along if needed. If getting married were a crime, we could easily be convicted of acting as accessories to marriage. Yes, officer, guilty as charged.

When I meet someone and the conversation turns to what I do for a living, as soon as that person hears that I'm a photographer, they automatically assume it means wedding photographer. (What other kind could there possibly be?) A small piece of my soul dies in that moment because I know that, if I had better applied myself,

I could be shooting covers for Harper's Bazaar by now. When I acknowledge that I do indeed spend my time photographing weddings, the person's eyes widen. Without even realizing it he or she grabs my arm and says, "Oh my God, I bet you see some crazy stuff. What's your wildest story?" Suddenly I'm put on the spot to spin an outlandish yarn.

Folks seem most interested in hearing about bridezillas. "Is that for real? Have you had any? Is it like what you see on TV?"

They are fascinated by the concept of a bride going berserk on her wedding day and want to know the dirt. Most of the awkward situations we have experienced don't actually involve the bride and groom. For the most part, we work with sane, emotionally stable, highly educated people who have friends and relatives who may be less sane or stable. So it's more like "friendzilla" or "Momzilla."

It's often the people and circumstances around the couples that make the stories: the drama queen grandmother, the cousin with lower-than-average self-awareness, the bystander who thinks they should be a part of the action just because they brought a gift, or the friend who has strong opinions about everything.

This cast of characters gives each wedding day its own personality. From the overbearing church lady to the uninvited guest, the mix of characters unknowingly join forces to create uncomfortable and hilarious situations.

No matter what the circumstances, our job is to create beautiful, memorable, and, above all, meaningful images for our clients. The kind that will make their friends jealous and their parents cry, that they will proudly show their grandkids someday. No matter what is going on around us, our purpose is to document our client's personal history and showcase them in the best way possible.

In order to provide full coverage and a comprehensive collection of images, I am given a great deal of access to the parts of the wedding day that the guests and most family never see. Being with the wedding couple for eight to fourteen hours, I'm often witnessing the unfiltered reality behind the scenes.

This collection of stories has been a hilarious trip down memory lane for me. We decided that it might be a good idea to change most of the names to protect the dignity of those involved. I guarantee you will laugh at least once and roll your eyes more than that. You might even gag once or twice (I know I did).

We could count on more than one hand the things we wish we had never seen, but there are plenty of stories we remember fondly. Luckily for us, we are usually observers who document the day. So it's not often that we are pulled directly into the drama. Having specialized in photographing weddings for more than a decade now, it can be easy to think that you've seen it all. Then next week's wedding proves you very, very wrong.

Chapter 1
The Cast of Characters

Weddings are theatrical events complete with a stage, a cast, wardrobe, props, a supportive crew backstage, and, of course, an audience. As with any production, the audience sees things as they were designed, with the actors playing out their roles and rarely breaking character. From the men in rented suits to the fancy rented cars to the hair styles that none of the women would wear in real life—everyone plays a character more elegant and sophisticated than themselves.

Backstage is a different story. Confrontation between cast members is common. Directors shout orders to the cast and crew, stage moms let everyone know that their baby should be getting more lines, and the lead actors feel under appreciated. The crew members roll their eyes and bite their tongues while putting two thumbs up and telling the cast that they're doing great. It's also worth pointing out that none of the actors are professionals and this play has only been loosely rehearsed one time on the previous evening.

It's true that many weddings are merely a theatrical event, though we've seen more than a few that seemed genuine and real. Those are the ones with handwritten vows and personal touches that honor the families and reflect the couple's personality. It also helps if no one takes the whole thing too seriously. They know that at the end of the evening, when the DJ plays "Last Dance" or "At Last" or, God forbid, that damn song by Journey that everyone loves so much, the couple goes away to begin a new life together. And that's the real prize.

Most weddings I have seen tend to play to the same tableaus that Disney movies put into little girls' heads twenty years earlier. As photographers, this can make our jobs easier at first, because we know what to expect. The princess and her prince spend a day with family going through a dozen or so formal rituals. They eventually do some line dances like the "Cupid Shuffle," or "Electric Slide," pump their fists to a Bon Jovi song or two, then escape through bubbles or sparklers and live happily ever after.

We've all seen that movie and a casual observer could make the mistake of thinking that, as artists, we photographers might get bored from the repetition. Ultimately, however, it doesn't matter how many times we see this movie play out; it's still our job to deliver photographs that make anyone believe the wedding was a perfect performance.

The following stories chronicle a few of our favorite characters and give a glimpse of what goes on backstage that the audience never gets to see.

The FOB

For us, the father of the bride is perhaps the most mysterious character at a wedding. Even though we are around him all day long, we rarely hear more than two or three words from him. He undoubtedly has a lot on his mind. Daddy's little girl is getting married; his wallet is tens, perhaps hundreds of thousands of dollars lighter. On top of that, he spends the entire day in an uncomfortable suit being nice to people he hardly knows.

He's also thinking about the father-daughter dance and the welcome speech he'll be giving at the reception. Should he wing it and speak from the heart, or read off of note cards to be sure all the bases are covered? Will he fumble during the speech? We have seen more than a few occasions where the FOB has called the groom by the wrong name during a welcome or a toast. It can be a lot of pressure to stand up in front of a crowded room where only half of the people look familiar; the FOB has to do it with sincerity and a smile.

At one wedding, our day began normally with a quaint ceremony at the family's church. The reception was across town, and our jaws dropped when we entered the ballroom. Surrounded by lavish decoration, every detail was exquisitely executed. The color pallet, the textures, theatrical lighting, the fine china, and the lead crystal were impressive. The visual experience could only be described as fabulously, insanely amazing (I usually hate using any of those words to describe something). Everything was the best of the best, and no expense had been spared. The floral arrangements were over the top, even by our standards. The food and entertainment were bigger, better, and finer than we had seen before.

We were in a tiny little town near Winston-Salem, North Carolina. But nearly all of the vendors, including us, traveled two hours from Raleigh. It's not like there is a lack of good wedding vendors in that area, so it struck us as curious.

It didn't take long to understand that this was not just a big deal wedding for the members of this community. It was *the* social event of the decade. The thing that friends, family, and business associates marked their calendars for, speculated about, agonized over what to wear, and gossiped about who would and would not be invited. It was also becoming obvious that the money spent on this carnival of opulence was to keep the guests impressed at every turn.

As the evening unfolded, we learned that Beth's father was one of the town's most respected businessmen, and many of his professional associates were in attendance. But we could also tell that he was a quiet type and was doing his best to grin and bear it through the day. The expression on his face confirmed that there were a dozen other places he would rather have been. Some FOBs are quiet because they feel a sense of loss or nostalgia over their little girl. Some are quiet because they know if they say or do anything stupid, their wife will kill them. Others just know to stay out of the way and let their girl be the star of the show, and that includes keeping quiet.

I did not interact with Beth's father until later in the evening. We found ourselves alone in the elevator going up to the ballroom. In an attempt to break the awkward silence that elevators tend to create, I commented that the day had gone flawlessly and asked him if he was relieved now that the toasts and the father-daughter dance were done.

Not missing a beat, he looked me in the eye. Without a bit of sarcasm he said, "Well, I feel like I just bought a new Mercedes and drove it straight into a lake."

Most Memorable Quotes Ever

"Dancing's a lot like sex, y'all. You don't have to be good at it to enjoy it. So everybody come on out to the dance floor!"

Swinging Richards Band

Uncle Frank

Once in a while an individual stands out as the life of the party. I'm not talking about the annoying guy that tries to get all the pretty girls out on the dance floor. I'm talking about that guest who breaks out from the crowd and delivers entertainment that gets the whole reception going nuts with frenzied people who are dancing and sweating more than they are used to and loving it. The result is a room filled with energy and people having such a great time that they want to stop for fear of hurting themselves but can't because it's so much fun. That lifetime achievement award goes without hesitation to Uncle Frank.

Photographically speaking, Joe and Katherine's was a picture perfect wedding. If you were to create a checklist for such a thing, it would read:

- Balmy spring weather
- Scenic location
- Gorgeous bride
- Horse-drawn carriage

- Groom with a fun-loving personality
- Flowers everywhere
- Attractive wedding party

It was quite the fairy tale and, following the ceremony, the whole group was ready for a good party. Southern receptions follow a fairly predictable format. The couple is introduced, the guests cheer them on, pretending it's the first time they've seen them together that day. They dance first with each other, then, if possible, the bride dances with her father and the groom with his mother. After that, a greeting is offered to guests, followed by a blessing for the meal. Dinner is served, and everyone gets a chance to catch his or her breath. After dinner, the band or the DJ attempts to get as many people out to the dance floor to get the "real party" started.

As far as we are concerned, the more people dancing the better our reception photos will be. The more people partying, the more we can photograph. If guests are having a great time, our images reflect that and our couples love to see photos of their guests enjoying themselves by acting crazy on the dance floor.

Joe and Katherine hired a band for their entertainment. We see a lot of great bands. They are usually booked out of Atlanta and are used to working the wedding crowds. They play timeless favorites that get the older crowd involved. Songs like "My Girl," "Sweet Caroline," and any sort of beach music. They also know when to crossover to get the younger crowd to "shake it like a Polaroid picture" with "Shout!" or "Celebration,"

But the band that Joe and Katherine booked was not that kind of band. They had never played a wedding before and were more used to playing in bars and clubs. The kind of band that sounded good belting out "Free Bird" but wouldn't be caught dead playing "The Way You Look Tonight." They were rock and roll, and so was the majority of the crowd. Meridith and I looked forward to seeing how this would go down.

The dancing was about what you'd expect from upper-middle-class white kids a few years out of college: straight out of the sorority and fraternity handbook actually. To my left I saw girls with hands in the air, head turned to the side, and rump shakin' down to the floor, followed by the frequent and obligatory tug on the top of the strapless dress to keep things classy. On my right, a groomsman with a drink in his hand was barely doing anything that looked like dancing. But it was okay because he was only a prop for the two bridesmaids grinding on either side of him. All of these are normal occurrences at most receptions.

That's when Uncle Frank took the stage. It was right after the band's first set. Joe and Katherine cut the cake, and we were ready for more of the party. Meridith and I heard whispers from the groomsmen that something fun was about to happen, something about an Uncle Frankie and the band. Not knowing what it was about, we figured whatever was going on would happen soon, so we stayed near the stage to catch it.

The band was in a little huddle to the side and then took their positions with their instruments. Frank was a big, burly dude, about six feet tall, and 280 pounds or more. He looked like the kind of guy I would not want to piss off for any reason. His coat and tie were long gone. With his cowboy boots and handlebar mustache he looked like he just rode in on his Harley to headline the show. Outside of my imagination, Frank was actually Joe's Uncle and seemed pretty cool for a badass.

Meridith came over and said, "Oh my God, that's the guy who told me that we are having a girl!" Meridith was about seven months pregnant at the time. Frank had approached her earlier and said he was a farmer, and could tell by the way she was carrying that the baby was a girl. He explained that he had a knack for predicting the gender of his farm animals' offspring by looking at how they carried the weight during pregnancy.

"The boys like to sprawl out and wrap their arms and legs round their momma, like a big ol' hug. So you would be carrying a lot wider. The girls just hang in there all folded up till they can get out, and so that's how I know you are having a little girl."

I looked at her with eyebrows raised. It was a fascinating concept, and I wanted to hear more. But just then the music started. It was go time for Frank's debut! The band started playing and what happened next was the best live rendition of "You Shook Me All Night Long" we have ever heard. This was no karaoke night down at the corner bar; it was high-energy entertainment. The crowd went completely nuts, with the whole place jumping up and down. Hair flying, heads banging, and fists pumping in the air, it was pure rock 'n roll. For two reprises lasting ten solid minutes, Frank had that crowd moving, jumping, sweating, pointing to the sky and shouting, "Hell to the yeah!" Young and old alike had caught the fever, and they had to have more of Uncle Frank.

Once the first song was over the crowd yelled for more, and Frank was happy to keep the party going. The band members looked at each other, shrugged as if to say, okay, whatever, and started up the next song. I think it was "Jessie's Girl." The only problem was that while the groomsmen were rocking out, they were also keeping Frank's glass full. By the fourth number, he had either forgotten most of the words to the songs or our ears stopped working right. I'm not sure that any of us knew what song we were supposed to be hearing. It didn't matter, though, because everyone else was as hammered as Frank, and they were probably hearing their own version of a different song in their heads. The remaining crowd stood close to the stage, swaying together with pained but sincere expressions on their faces. Holding beers high in the air, they agreed with Frank that every single one of us is indeed "living on a prayer."

We could tell that the band was ready to get back to the previously scheduled program and see their lead singer reclaim his spot on stage.

"At some point this is going to get old," I said to Meridith.

"Yeah, about ten minutes ago," she responded.

To this day we still talk about Uncle Frank and how great those first few moments were. The energy he created by stepping on stage is not something you can rehearse. It happens on its own, and magic is created. Of course, the moral of the story is also to realize that while magic can happen, it's not sustainable for more than one or two songs.

And it turns out Frank was right: we had a girl!

Bridezilla

People ask us about "bridezillas" all the time, as if she really is some larger-than-life mythical creature that stomps around weddings and eats skyscrapers. While I'm sure she is lurking out there somewhere, we have only caught brief glimpses of this creature. Barring all of the so-called reality TV shows that showcase the bridezilla, she is far from a common thing to see. Of the hundreds of weddings we have photographed, we have only witnessed a half-dozen or so brides who qualify for the bridezilla label. That's around 1 percent, for anyone who likes statistics.

One of the problems is that everyone has a different opinion of what you have to do to be considered a bridezilla. It goes beyond a tendency to be generally bitchy or whiny or bossy. We often see those traits, but we wouldn't slap a b-zilla sticker on those brides. Some people are just bitchy, whiny, and bossy all the time, whether they're wearing a big white dress or yoga pants. Maybe I have a high tolerance for outbursts, but wedding days can be stressful. Everyone reacts differently to stress, and you can't smack a label on them just because they speak (or sometimes scream) before they think.

Being stressed is one thing, but a true bridezilla is the one who is the source of stress, both for herself and those around her. She puts everyone on edge and makes them miserable. Close family and bridesmaids become so afraid to upset the apple cart that they hang back and don't say or do much. Then, when the bride yells at them for not helping or participating, they shut down even further. There is an obvious pattern that develops, but you see it only in hindsight. We have never been able to predict who will turn into this mythical bridezilla creature until we see the disaster unfolding for ourselves. The ones you think are completely sane will surprise you with a momentary glimpse of their potential b-zilla when it's least expected.

In each case we have witnessed, the bride seemed fine one moment and then just snapped Jekyll-and-Hyde style. It's the most common trait of the bridezilla: you never know when she will snap and who will be the target. Once we saw a bride gaze lovingly into her new husband's eyes while we photographed them just after the ceremony. Three seconds later, she slapped him for "not smiling right for the camera" and stormed away. We stood there dumbfounded. Later we learned that the groom had undergone oral surgery two weeks earlier, and it hurt when he smiled. I wonder if they're still together.

In every case, the anger was directed at a close family member. Most of the time we see moms get the biggest dose of bridezilla rage. It's weird because she's usually a nice, quiet, little lady who just wants everything in the world to be right for her little girl. If she makes one suggestion too much, out come the fangs and bridezilla goes for the throat. Then as quickly as the fangs came out they go back again, and everybody pretends that all is normal and that ridiculous fit never happened. All the while, the mangled corpse of her mother's fragile emotions lay on the floor bleeding for everyone in the room to see.

Of course, these outbursts take place in front of us, but I can tell that the bride convinces herself that we didn't see or hear it. Maybe she thinks that we were looking the other way, or because we had a camera in front of our faces, we were somehow shielded from exposure to her childishness. The bride is in denial that she acted in such an immature and hateful manner to someone who only wants the day to go well. Everyone (including us) plays along as if that were true. It's like she had a hateful convulsion and then in the snap of a finger woke up wondering if it really happened. She quickly convinces herself it did not.

Another commonality among bridezillas is the expectation that this single day is going to be the most perfect and amazing day of their lives. Everything should move like clockwork and everyone should be in their places and not ask the bride silly questions. In other words, these brides are often perfectionists with incredibly unrealistic expectations of those around them. They have spent their whole lives planning and living for their wedding day, and hell shall rain down on the poor souls who dare wake her from the dream. That is a lot of pressure to place on yourself and those around you, never mind being completely impractical. These are the girls who scream at their sister: "I don't need thinkers, I need foot soldiers, damn it!"

Before and after the wedding day the bridezillas we have encountered were typically sweet and soft-spoken. We still can't make the call on who will snap. Sometimes we meet with a bride who seems more rigid than most about her wedding day plans. Meridith and I glance at each other with an expression that asks, Could this be the one? If we're ever able to identify the warning signs, that will be a book all by itself.

Most Memorable Quotes Ever

"Come on y'all, this is my first weddin'. I want it to be beautiful."

Bride pleading to her parents after they suggested cutting back on the flower budget.

Oh Wait, You're Famous?

I live in North Carolina, which is not known as a hot bed of the entertainment world. We do however have several high profile universities in the area. When we work with clients who are "celebrities," they tend to be from the sports or political worlds. The trouble is the average preschooler knows more about quantum physics than I know about sports and sports figures, so it's easy for me to look stupid when talking to people who take this stuff seriously.

At one meeting with a potential bride, she brought her mother, future mother-in-law, and the groom's aunt. A bit odd, but not totally out of the ordinary. We exchanged pleasantries and talked about photos.

As the meeting was winding down, the groom's mom leaned toward me and said, "We like what you do. We just want to make sure that you can be discreet because of my son's situation."

Until that point, the groom had never been mentioned, and I had no idea what this "situation" was. You can bet that my mind went a thousand different directions at once. Was he on the run, maybe in witness protection? Maybe he received a terminal diagnosis, or was he some dot-com tycoon, or on a terrorist watch list?

My curiosity was dialed up to level ten. Trying to play it cool, I nodded my head and said, "Well sure. I just want to make sure I fully understand his...situation." I said it as if expecting some elaborate story that would include a Russian spy named Nadia and plot twists that would decide the fate of our very existence.

"He plays ball," she replied.

A long pause followed as I struggled to reconcile what she just said with the gravity of the circumstances I had anticipated. I was thinking, "He plays ball. What in the ever loving hell does that mean and what about that qualifies as a situation?" I was also thinking, "James, get that stupid, confused expression off your face. They are right there and can see you! Go back to smiling!" That's when they told me his name, and they just wanted to be sure that I wouldn't plaster his photos all over the place after the wedding.

Still a little confused, I had given up on trying to be cool. His name didn't sound remotely familiar, so I decided to just ask the question. The room was dead silent with four people staring at me. It seemed like an eternity to get the words out.

I said, "So, he plays...football?"

They all chuckled. To my relief, I could tell they liked that I had no idea about the groom's celebrity status. They explained that he played basketball. I think it was for the New York Knicks at that time. They were really great people. We shot the wedding and learned a little more about basketball. It also reinforced for me that people appreciate when you treat them professionally and avoid making a big deal about who they are or what they do.

Those who are more visible in society are usually cool about it. They treat people respectfully and work well with fans and gawkers alike. It's the people who want to have some fame, or who happen to have a semifamous person in the wedding party who "get a little big for their britches" (that's a Southern expression, y'all).

As in the case above, it's good to know what kind of situation we're walking into before the wedding day so we can make a plan for how to handle it. Sometimes we aren't that lucky, though. Many years ago, a couple we worked with had a typical country-club wedding. Unless you have a great planner, these events can fall into a predictable pattern. This wedding was elegant without being pretentious, yet somehow managed to be devoid of any of the couple's personality. I called it the vanilla wedding because there was so little for us to photograph.

When we arrived, however, their planner told me a few of the groomsmen were NBA players. One in particular was a hometown hero type that the guests would go crazy over at the reception. I couldn't tell which ones were the ball players, because while the groom was maybe five feet eight inches tall, everyone else seemed eight feet tall and athletic looking. Aside from wishing I had a ladder because I felt so damn short, we went about the day taking pictures as if it were any client in front of our cameras. Three hours into the day, I still didn't know which ones were supposedly famous.

The guys were totally relaxed and a pleasure to work with. The bride, Nikki, on the other hand was a bit high-strung. Based on the instructions she was giving on the phone when we arrived to see her, I could tell that she had spent a great deal of time envisioning scenarios in which crazed sports fans would bust through the doors in the middle of her ceremony in search of an autograph. She also told her bridesmaids that she was afraid there would be issues with her own invited guests bothering the best man by lining up to talk to him or asking to pose for pictures.

After the ceremony at Nikki's family church, Meridith and I made our way to the country club to set up for the reception. As we were about to enter the club, we were stopped by two security guards who asked for our business cards and identification. They checked our name against the list on their clipboard and let us in.

"Is the President coming to dinner?" I asked Meridith, "Or is this girl completely out of touch with reality?"

She actually hired security guards to stand at the entrance of the country club, as if paparazzi were going to tear through the walls of the place. These weren't your off duty police officer security people either. With muscles bulging through their black t-shirts that said SECURITY on the back, they looked more like nightclub bouncers.

The reception progressed, and I began noticing a hint of negative energy from some of the guests directed toward me. A few wouldn't smile for a group photo, while others seemed to be scowling at me. Some people don't like to have their pictures taken, I thought to myself. Then later, when photographing an older couple on the dance floor it happened again. When the guy saw my camera, he seemed annoyed and waved me off. He mumbled something that I couldn't hear because of the music, but I figured that maybe he was there with his mistress and didn't want pictures of them floating out in the world.

Two hours into the party, Meridith came up to me and said that she just overheard Nikki telling a group of guests, "It's in the photographer's contract they are the only ones allowed to take any photos." She was telling the guests that we had security there to enforce this rule, and she asked them to please put their cameras away so they didn't get in trouble.

No wonder people were scowling at us. The bride had been around the whole room lying to everyone and saying that we were prohibiting guests from taking pictures of her. It could not have been further from the truth. The reality was that she did not like to have her picture taken and wanted to control who had images of her. She made us modify our contract to say that we would not use her wedding photos on websites, blogs, or anywhere else. That part didn't upset me at all. But I knew she was hard core when a year after the wedding I received a call from her mother asking if there was any way I could show her a few pictures because Nikki would not share them with her or anyone in the family.

Still speechless from the realization that we were being vilified by our client to her friends and family in the middle of her reception, Meridith and I huddled in the corner assessing our potential PR disaster.

"What do we do?" Meridith asked. "She doesn't want people to take her picture, but now they're mad at us!"

I'm known to be pretty level-headed in tense situations, but there's only so much I can handle before I toss decorum out the window. When that happens a guy named Jimmy shows up. You know that part of your personality that just doesn't care what other people think? That side of you that sees the six-year-old kid screaming at his mom in the grocery store and feels compelled to go punch him in the throat? We all have that person living inside us. I call mine Jimmy.

"Let's go tell each end every person in this room that Nikki is a complete nut job and they are free to take all the pictures they want!" I said.

Being the wiser of the two of us, Meridith urged, "I don't think that will improve our situation."

"Then forget it. I'll stand beside her for the last hour and a half of this thing waiting for someone to ask me to take their picture. I'll be sure to only keep the ones where she blinks!"

As Meridith and I sparred in the corner of the ballroom, our bride was hatching a new plan. As much as Nikki wanted a lovely wedding, it was becoming obvious that she also wanted as little contact with her guests as possible. Her mother wouldn't let her go sit it out at the bar, and there was no way she was going out on the dance floor, so she decided to leverage her wedding party to divert attention away from herself. She set up a spot at the far end of the room where guests could stand and pose for pictures with their famous NBA friend. She told everyone that it was fine to use their cameras for pictures with him and that he would autograph their wedding program. Nikki was an evil genius indeed, because her plan worked. The poor guy stood there for nearly an hour shaking hands, cheesing for the cameras, and pretending to be interested in whatever people were saying to him. All the while, Nikki hung out on the other end of the ballroom with her bridesmaids.

After the wedding, I never brought it up to Nikki that we were aware of what she told her guests about us. It didn't matter though, because I only heard from her one time after her wedding day. I delivered her proofs, and she reminded me not to let anyone see her pictures. After all these years I have heard from her mom a few times telling us that she loved all the photos she has seen and wants us to print some pictures for her. But Nikki does not return calls or emails. Oh well.

The Trouble with Horses

Horses don't bother me as long as I don't have to be near them. Many see them as beautiful and majestic creatures; I see them as big, scary animals that can't communicate their feelings well. I don't dislike them; I'm just never really confident whether I'll be safe or stomped, or licked or kicked. Having horses as part of a wedding is one of those things that seems like a great idea. I guess it brings that fairy princess element to the event. Whether they are pulling a carriage or just in the pasture as a part of the scenic backdrop, horses can certainly set the mood and help create a dramatic entrance or exit.

They can be good at killing the mood too. Even with top trainers and skilled handling, they have minds of their own, and that can make for unpredictable situations. We have had several interesting experiences with horses at weddings. Some made us think we would die laughing, and a few made us think we might actually die for real.

Amanda was getting married on the front lawn of her parents' estate and decided a horse-drawn carriage would deliver her to the aisle for her ceremony. Two white horses pulled a proper carriage that looked straight out of any storybook you have ever read involving princesses. It was sure to meet the approval of even the most snobbish wedding guest. Behind the manor, out of sight of the seated guests and wedding party, Amanda's father helped her into the carriage. They waited for their signal.

Once the guests were settled into their seats, the string quartet began to play and the wedding director gave the sign for the horses to begin moving. The coachmen, dressed in formal English riding garb, pulled around the side of the grounds. You could hear the gasps as the guests sitting in the lawn at the front of the manor saw the fairy tale scene playing out in front of them. The strings played on and the carriage pulled up to the end of the aisle runner with flawless execution. Amanda's father stepped down and helped hold her flowers and dress as a coachman also assisted in helping her to the ground. The guests rose to their feet and Amanda locked eyes with Jim as she walked down the aisle to get married.

The music was still playing and the carriage pulled away so that there was no chance of the horses getting restless and disturbing the ceremony. The plan was for the wedding director to signal for it to return just before the newlyweds kissed and walked back up the aisle. For the next twenty minutes, my attention was focused on creating emotional imagery of the bride and groom facing each other on the steps in front of me.

The ceremony went exactly as planned and was nearing its conclusion. I was concentrating on getting the best angle for the kiss and barely noticed that the horses had pulled up just a few feet behind me at the end of the aisle. I made a note that they were behind me so I didn't get too close and went back to shooting the last few details of the ceremony. The minister said, "Let us pray," and I knew the next thing was the kiss, and then Amanda and Jim would walk toward me through a crowd of cheering people.

Five seconds into the prayer, as everyone was silent with heads bowed, I heard the strangest noise. I looked behind me in the direction of the noise and saw two guys on the back row with their hands over their faces laughing hysterically. The sound was muffled but noticeable as they were doubled over and uncontrollable. My first thought was "How rude. What the hell could be so funny during a prayer? I'm right here in the middle of everything, and if anything funny happened I would have seen it or heard it." A split second later, I turned around further and saw the source of both their laughter and the noise that I was hearing.

I really don't think that any guests near the front could hear it. I know that the entire wedding party was oblivious to it. But the horse closest to me was completely emptying his bladder right there at the end of the aisle during the prayer. If you've ever seen a horse do this, you know it goes on for quite a while.

It doesn't happen often, but I completely lost my composure. I had to walk away, far away from the guests and put my arm over my face to hold it all in. I was laughing to the point of choking and convulsions because I was trying to be quiet and not attract attention. Hysteria turned to worry as my method for suppressing my laugh was also depriving me of oxygen. I thought I might pass out any second. Even though I knew that two very important photo opportunities were about to happen, I just could not collect myself. The rushing water sound finally stopped as the prayer drew to a close, and as liquid always does, it began running down hill in the direction of the guests. I'm sure the horse felt relieved because he created quite a large puddle at the exact spot where Jim and Amanda would be walking next.

At that moment I was thankful for four things: I was thankful that the minister was long-winded and that during the lengthy prayer I could return to being semifunctional. Once he pronounced the couple married, I was thankful that the camera fully covers my face when shooting, because I was still laughing my ass off and had tears rolling down my cheeks. Third, I was thankful for the recessional music and applause, which gave me the necessary camouflage to laugh out loud from behind my camera and stop choking. Finally, I was thankful that the camera had great auto focus because I couldn't really see a thing anymore.

Through all of that, I still got the important shots. Both the kiss and the smiling couple walking toward me up the aisle and getting into the carriage. It seemed that no one had a clue what had happened during the prayer except the few folks in the back row. As Amanda and Jim passed me and got closer to the puddle, a coachman moved forward and guided them around it so smoothly that they never noticed. It took me a full hour and several ginger ales to recover from that ordeal.

A completely different wedding had us shooting out in the country for Julie and Kyle. They were having the entire event on her parents' horse farm. The scenery was straight out of a Timberlake painting (not that Timberlake, I'm talking about Bob; look him up). It was late May and the weather could not have been nicer. Flowers were blooming, breezes were blowing, and the sun was shining. There were pastures, barns, rustic fences, gravel roads, and, of course, several horses.

As we often do during outdoor ceremonies, Meridith and I took opposite sides of the aisle and worked our way around the perimeter for the best angles. We try to keep our distance and be discreet so we don't distract the guests during the ceremony.

The processional began, and Julie was glowing beautifully as the sunlight filtered through the trees and struck her veil. To the left of the ceremony area was the horse pasture. As the minister began the greetings and vows, a few horses wandered up to the fence to see what all the fuss was about and why so many people were on their farm.

Somewhere between the vows and the ring exchange, I remember moving around to get a better angle on the parents and grandparents sitting on the front row. It makes for good pictures to see them looking at each other, shedding a tear, or expressing any sort of emotion. As I was getting into position, Kyle was beginning to recite his vows to Julie. In the middle of his part, the loud, explosive sound of horsey gas echoed through the valley.

Instead of taking photos of Mom wiping away tears, I was getting people looking to the person beside them with the expression that said, "Did you hear that too? Was that what I think it was? Did that really just happen? Well, it wasn't me!"

Then came the laughter. Not out loud. This was polite, suppressed laughter: hand over your mouth, close your eyes, rock forward, and hope your ears don't pop.

When the bride and groom are up at the altar during the ceremony, they go into a zone, a trance-like state. They neither see nor hear anything except for the minister who is feeding them their lines. Because of this phenomenon, when things disrupt the ceremony, the couple is completely unaware of it.

It was so entertaining to observe middle-aged folks who were dressed in their fancy clothes overtaken by the giggles because a horse broke wind during the wedding ceremony. If Julie and Kyle had looked back at the audience at that moment, they would have seen tears and big smiles on most of the faces. They naturally would have thought that all of those people were happy for them, but the real reason was far more entertaining.

For some couples, it's important that they have a memorable exit. A grand send off that lets all of the guests know that the bride and groom are leaving, the party is over, and they are free to go home. This is the part of the day where we sometimes see too many elements and expectations get packed into the exit. Of all of the romantic notions related to horses at weddings, one of the most popular seems to be the horse and carriage send-off. A send-off through sparklers and a carriage get away sounds down right enchanting, doesn't it?

In reality, when handing sixty to a hundred drunken folks a sparkler and crowding them around a horse-drawn carriage, it's a safe bet that something bad will happen. It seems like such a good idea until you witness it go completely wrong. It was the end of the evening at a wedding in Atlantic Beach, and the guests had thoroughly enjoyed the party, especially the bar area.

It was time for the couple to make their getaway. The carriage, which was pulled by two very stout horses, was settled under the portico. I took a few photos and waited for the guests to filter out. Five minutes later, I was in the midst of chaos with a crowd of rowdy people packed into a small space, shoulder to shoulder and waving glowing hot metal sticks while surging toward the carriage and spooking the horses.

I was stuck between one of the horses and the wheel of the carriage, frantically looking for an exit. There were cars parked in front of the horses and people on all sides of me. There was no way out, and I began to panic. As more people pressed against me, the horses started squealing and bucking. I looked up at the coachmen, both with expressions of horror on their faces. Realizing that they were about to lose control, they gripped the reigns with everything they had.

The couple emerged from the building and ran through the gauntlet while dodging the pyrotechnics. The crowd went wild and became even louder with cheering and sparkler waving. Everything was completely out of control, and I had nowhere to go. Trapped between a large, scared animal and a hundred unruly people with fire in their hands, you begin to reevaluate your life.

The horses squealed again and reared up on their hind legs, bucking to get the hell out of there. It was then that I made peace with the situation and realized I was part of something very special. Because in that moment it hit me that of all of my friends, I'll have the most interesting story about how I died.

White Collar Prisons

In our line of work, it's more common to be around people who are wealthy than those who might be considered famous. It's generally assumed that if someone is famous then they are probably well off financially. But there is an endless list of people you've never heard of who are loaded with cash. Being as close as we are to the cast of characters during a wedding-day performance, we have the benefit of catching some thought provoking conversations.

It's fascinating to hear what people choose to talk about in social situations. Their views of the world and money are shaped significantly by how they earned their wealth in the first place. For most of the men we see, you can divide their wealth into two broad categories: old money and new money.

Those guys that started their business back in 1962 and built it from the ground up; that's old money. The twenty-eight-year-old who has been living off his late Daddy's fortune for the better part of his adult life, that too is old money. Contrast that with the newly successful professionals. The doctor, attorney, stockbroker, athlete, musician who have put in their ten thousand hours, paid their dues, and are just beginning to see the rewards of their efforts. That's new money. Often they're at a place in their career where the cash is rolling in and they are struggling to figure out what to do with it all.

Old money isn't as interested in fancy cars or trophy wives. They talk mostly about their leisure pursuits. You'll likely hear them discussing recent vacation adventures, their latest charity event, and, of course, their escapades either on the golf course or the tennis court, depending on gender. It's all rather civilized and uninteresting.

New money on the other hand feels like they're finally living life! No more small apartments and ramen noodles. Now it's all Bentleys and Rolexes. They don't talk about golf, either. New money discussions are filled with colorful topics that tend to center around two main themes.

1. Other people with money
2. Crazy ways to make more money

That's where things get interesting, because if I have to be hanging out in a hotel suite for an hour taking photos of guys putting on bow ties and struggling to figure out how cuff links work, I don't care as much about where you went on your last vacation. I am, however, fascinated to hear you try to convince the other groomsmen in the room how you think you can double your money over two years by investing in bioengineered alpaca farms.

When I walked into one groom's suite to photograph him preparing and accessorizing, I knew right away that the vibe in the room was lively and would soon get interesting. There were probably five other guys in the suite, and they were all picking on one guy for owning a pair of denim shorts. These guys "played ball" and the conversation went from 1986 jean shorts to how none of them would ever want to be as famous as LeBron James.

"He couldn't even take his kids to Disney World without people swarming all over him. I can put on some sun glasses and get by most people, but LeBron's screwed!"

Side conversations started breaking out as the men were going into different rooms to get into their suits. Two groomsmen remained in the living room area and talked about their latest adventures in investing.

"My neighbor was telling me about this thing his accountant told him. You can invest in building private prisons. Thing is, you own part of the actual prison like a piece of real estate, and the government pays you to keep their prisoners there. It's a sure thing, 'cause the government's prisons are already overcrowded, and they don't have a budget to build more. You just gotta make sure it's one of those minimum security deals. Accountant said those are cheaper to run because they don't take as many guards, and you don't need as many fences around it. It's the kinda place where they send white-collar guys like embezzlers and the stock-market swindler types. It's a sure thing year in and year out 'cause the world never runs out of criminals"

As I moved into the adjoining room to photograph the groom suiting up, the conversation shifted from unconventional investment ideas to the locker room talk that is far more customary in the groom's suite. Tales of girlfriends past yielded this sage advice from one groomsman: "You know any girl worth havin' has had them legs thrown over another dude's shoulders at some point, so you gotta look past that." He didn't seem to be talking to anyone in particular, but everyone in the room nodded in agreement with this pearl of wisdom.

Even though I never know what to expect from one wedding to the next, there's a good chance I'll walk away knowing more than I did walking in that day.

Uncle Bob

I was going to mention Uncle Bob in the list of wedding code words you'll read about soon, but this guy deserves a whole section of the book. Uncle Bob is a character present at every wedding we do. He's not a specific person, but more like a kind of person. In fact, his name is not really Bob. It could be John or Norman or Chuck, but we call him Uncle Bob. There have even been a few weddings that had more than one Uncle Bob in the crowd.

In the wedding photography world, "Uncle Bob" is code for a guy with a nice camera who knows enough about photography to be dangerous and thinks he could easily handle my job. These are the guys who want to talk about cameras and compare megapixels. They are often impressed when they see the big lens on our cameras and will comment on it or ask us about it. Bob wouldn't be caught dead taking pictures with his phone like the rest of the guests. That's what the common folk use. He opts instead for a nice middle-of-the-line consumer model that looks like it could be too complicated for his wife to want to use it.

Bobs come in all ages, though I find that older Uncle Bobs like to talk about the good old days of film and how "you had to know what you were doing back then." As if somehow you don't anymore. I have also photographed enough traditional Korean ceremonies to know that everyone around you is Uncle Bob. I used to get jealous when I saw the groom's dad or the bride's uncle packing the latest, greatest Gadgetron-9000 professional series camera, looking at me like, "yeah, I'm bad, I know it." As years have passed, I've matured a lot, though. I've overcome my camera envy by internalizing my insecurities and later expressing them through passive-aggressive status updates on Facebook.

I've also found that the serious Uncle Bobs all seem to be dentists. What's with that? If there is a guy at a wedding who has a nicer camera than mine and that guy is not Korean, then there is a four out of five chance that he is a dentist. If he is Korean, it's still safe to bet that he's also a dentist.

Even my own dentist has a photo studio set up in his office, and when I go in for a cleaning we end up talking about the latest cameras and software. I still haven't made the connection between what dentists do in their daily routine that compels them to create photographs. I'm going to have to explore that one more. I'll be sure to put that on the to-do list.

Most often Bob is laid back and only chats a little. Sometimes though, it seems like he has something to prove. The ones I remember most are competitive and go out of their way to show us up. At one wedding there was a Bob who was all up in our personal space for most of the time before and during the ceremony. He was in the aisle during the vows and generally everywhere he could be to either block a shot or be in one. He was snapping photos the whole time and had the motor drive going like he was shooting the one-hundred-meter dash at the Olympics! This was the freaking ring exchange—not exactly a high-speed event.

Accessory to Marriage

After the ceremony, he was right in there at our shoulders during the family photos just snapping away. This guy didn't know when to leave it alone and subtlety was not a concept he was aware of. I could tell that he knew that he was making our jobs difficult, and he seemed proud of it. Making our lives difficult also meant an uncomfortable experience and fewer images for his relative, the bride. I think he was the groom's uncle, so I practiced patience and refrained from snapping his neck right there in church.

Once the family photos were complete, Meridith and I were finally alone with the couple for a few minutes. It was great! We had peace and quiet and no other happy snappers around. Uncle Bob was nowhere in sight. It was both wonderful and disconcerting, and I kept anticipating that he would jump out from behind the bushes any second. At the reception there was time for us to work with the couple and their wedding party before the introductions. I was both relieved and confused to see that Uncle Bob was still absent. All of the stress of the previous few hours melted away, and we were able to do the job we were brought there for with no interruptions.

Even when we got into the reception area where Uncle Bob should have been enjoying a cocktail, we did not see him. This was a complete change from what we had experienced the first half of the day, when he was all over us. Once dinner started, it all became clear when Uncle Bob strolled in with three books under his arm and proceeded to monopolize the attention of the head table by passing around the "wedding albums" that he had just produced at the drug store on the way to the reception.

You could see his chest all puffed out and the look on his face could have gone right beside the dictionary definition of the words *self-satisfied.* He looked over at us with that look that said, "Losers! Look what I can do." The couple was trying so hard to seem both interested and grateful for such an odd gesture. You could tell by their expressions they were searching for nice things to say, but their body language suggested that they would rather get on with their meal.

Later in the evening I had an opportunity to sneak a glance at the books. The photos in their lovely, simulated cowhide vinyl flipbooks were just average snapshots and nothing really special or creative. I realize that sounds petty for me to say that, but I have to admit feeling relieved about it. If they had been wonderful images that captured emotion or depicted a stirring narrative, then I would have felt defeated. What I saw were snapshots taken over my shoulder, and it made me feel good that what I would be delivering to that newly married couple in a few weeks was vastly different, even though it was a photo of the same thing taken at the same time.

Most of the time we play well with Uncle Bob. We actually call him Bob throughout the day, which throws him off a little. Next time you're at a wedding and need something to pass the time, see if you can spot Uncle Bob. Ask him about his camera and lens and megapixels too. Even if you don't know what any of it means, Bob will entertain you with his answers.

Behind the Scenes Insight

Jimmy Code

There's a voice inside my brain that is rude and judgmental. It's a lot like having two completely opposite personalities that share an affinity for wearing black button-down shirts. This voice is constantly screaming at me to let the world experience its hard truths, but I know that would end badly. I call the voice Jimmy, and he hasn't quite grasped the benefits of being sensitive to feelings, having language filters, empathy, or any of that new-age hippy crap. He loves the F-word and often uses it as every word in a sentence. Jimmy just tells it like it is, and the whole conversation takes place inside of my head. Most of the time I do a pretty good job of suppressing Jimmy, but every once in a while his biting sarcasm can slip past my brain and out of my mouth. Not many people have met him. It's simply not good for business. If you ever get the chance, well, I apologize in advance.

Jimmy's cynical and toxic rants have even inspired a full vocabulary of code words that Meridith and I use at every wedding. Besides helping us express frustration or amusement right out in the open without naming names, these code words also help pass information quickly without really elaborating about the specifics of a person or situation; for example, whom to keep an eye on for the action, or whom to avoid. Meridith and I often arrive to a wedding wired up with two-way radios and little earpieces that make us look like Secret Service agents. Having that is cool enough by itself. Throw in some code words, and now we're on a totally different level, one that qualifies us for our own secluded tree fort in the woods, complete with a secret handshake. Using Jimmy's codes helps us to be faster, to be more aware of our surroundings, to get better angles, and to have more fun than if we spoke using lots of boring words. Here are some examples of our codes:

Triple-D (Drunk Dude Dancing)—This is the one guy at a party who's gotten his fill of liquid courage, and now he's going to show off *all* his dance moves. He usually makes an appearance about two-thirds of the way through the reception, when most people who are on the dance floor with him are equally hammered. Once we know which guy is going to end up being that evening's Triple-D, we lock our cameras on him in anticipation of a great show. Maybe he'll start with a little lawnmower or the grocery cart, but when you see him and his date do the fish-on-a-hook bit, you know that the robot is not far behind. After the crowd is worked up and forms a big circle around him, he'll finish out the routine with the worm as the grand finale.

Fluffy—That one bridesmaid who won't let the bride move six freaking inches without leaning over to adjust the dress and spread it evenly around. Every wedding has a fluffy. These ladies can be super annoying because they are so worried about the dress that they ignore everything else around them. As I am working to create images that capture natural expressions of the bride, I constantly catch Fluffy's big butt in the corner of the photo bending over to adjust the dress. For Fluffy, it's not good enough to just obsess over the dress being straight. She is also the one who appoints herself worrier-in-chief regarding all things nature-related that could potentially damage the dress. Once I was working with a bride and her bridesmaids outside just before the ceremony. Fluffy had the bottom of the bride's dress spread out perfectly on the grass, even though I told her I wasn't going to photograph below the waist. I had everyone placed and was walking over to adjust my light before making the first photo. As I reached the light and was adjusting the power on the flash, I heard Fluffy yell, "RAIN!" When I looked back at the group, everyone had abandoned me. They were hurrying back inside the church to avoid the impending monsoon. Only there was no rain. It never rained at all that day, but thanks to Fluffy we missed out on a ton of great memories. Now, whenever we identify a fluffy, we make sure that she has plenty of other stuff to hold, carry, or errands to run (for the bride, of course) to keep her from ruining our photos.

Sparkles—The person who either blinks a lot or tries to avoid blinking by anticipating when you will take the photo. This causes a strained expression on their face resembling shock or surprise. Whenever I spot Sparkles in a crowd, I know I'll be taking four or five times more pictures than normal, just to get that one where Sparkles looks awake and completely lucid. I wonder why there's always one in a wedding party. Maybe Sparkles' mom ruined him or her as a child with all of her happy snapping. With any luck, I identify Sparkles early in the day and get lots of photos, knowing that 90 percent will be deleted due to blinking.

Crazy SOB (Sister(s) of the Bride)—Not all SOBs are crazy, most are quite delightful. But you occasionally get the one who was just married two years before Little Sis and knows how all of this photo stuff should go down. Add in a tendency to be dramatic or controlling and you have a recipe for someone to be avoided at all costs. Luckily, it's easy to tell which ones are going to be crazy. They usually seek us out to say, "I'm not going to be crazy or controlling. I just want my Sister's day to be perfect for her, and I have a few ideas based on what happened at my wedding." I can count on more than one hand the brides who spent the day having to remind her sister whose wedding day it actually was.

Pit butt—The unhappy bulge that occurs at the armpit of most strapless-dress-wearing women. If you think it only happens to the curvy girls, think again. Pitt-butt can happen regardless of fitness level. Because a proper lady would never accept the skin under her arm bulging from the top of her gown, I am often asked to retouch this phenome-non. To do this I have to zoom into the area so that it fills my screen. I then work to make the curved line of the bulge straighter and lighten the delicate shadows so the area looks flat. If someone walked behind me and saw my screen before I begin working on this area, they would swear they were seeing a photo of some person's bare ass.

It really is a vicious cycle. So many women want strapless gowns. But with them comes concerns about the dress slipping, so an attempt is made to thwart gravity by making the top a little tighter. Then any skin under the arms spills out and bulges over the top. Posture has a lot to do with the severity of the bulge. But only ballet dancers and fashion models know how awesome it looks to stand up straight anymore. So we try giving gentle posture suggestions before employing other methods to minimize the dreaded PB. There are only two real cures for it, and neither involves a diet. The first and most effective would be for a bride to **wear a dress with straps**! There, I said it. The second is for her to have a nice long veil that we can use to cover up the arm, thus hiding the tiny butt from view.

While pit butt is only slightly more prevalent in full-figured women, it can strike most anyone. Ultimately though, it's a far better situation than what the really skinny girls have to endure. You'll read about the problems fashion models face soon enough.

PG (Photo Guy)—There's always at least one single guy at the reception who acts interested in photography and wants to ask Meridith about her camera and big lens. We call him Photo Guy. Don't confuse him with Uncle Bob. These are two totally different characters. Uncle Bob just wants to take pictures. PG couldn't care less about photography. He doesn't even have a camera. He only talks to Meridith because she's pretty and seems approachable, and PG is at the wedding looking to score somehow. Meridith used to get annoyed by this and direct them to see me about camera-related stuff, which he never did. PG doesn't want to talk to a guy. That's not what he's there to accomplish.

In recent years Meridith is more willing to mess with PG, throwing out nonsensical technical info. If you are Photo Guy and walk up seeing her holding a camera that obviously says Canon on the front, then ask her, "What kind of camera you working with there?" she might answer, "It's an Axitron 7300 with night vision and twenty frames-per-second auto arm slimming." None of that exists or even makes sense, but it will make PG walk away scratching his head.

Fashionable—Whenever Jimmy calls someone fashionable, it means he or she is late. The best thing is that you can say it right to somebody's face aı ıd most everyone will take it as a compliment. Others just look at you like you're strange. I'm okay with that too. Our most fashionable bride ever was just under two hours late for her own ceremony. Her hair person couldn't get the extensions to look exactly the way they discussed a few weeks earlier, so our bride sat there in the hotel as though she had nowhere to be while guests across town at the ceremony were treated to two hours of the same six wedding songs from the organist. Jimmy likes late people about as much as he likes being stung by jellyfish or having his body waxed while listening to Journey's greatest hits (threw up a little just typing those last three words).

Aunt Sally—A similar yet more tenacious counterpart to Uncle Bob. Aunt Sally doesn't care that she's all up in my Cheese Whiz while I'm trying to shoot. Most Bobs at least respect my personal space, but not Sally. She wants to be right at my shoulder or, more often, being around five feet tall, she's at my armpit, which is unnerving. Unlike Bob, who is just there to take pictures of what is already happening, Sally is far more excited about all of the wonderful photographic possibilities, and she's there to make memories happen. If I'm not careful, she will push me out of the way and take control of the session. She'll begin instructing the bride and groom to pose for her while making me wait my turn. If she is not actually taking photos, then she's sure to be super helpful and suggest all sorts of poses and family combinations that we should be taking. Once in the middle of a father-daughter dance, an Aunt Sally, armed with her camera phone, asked Meridith, "Can you move out of the way so I can get this?" We don't get aggressive Sallies often, but when we do it turns into a very long day. Jimmy hasn't punched Aunt Sally so far, but he can't rule it out completely.

Episcopalian—This code word is applied liberally to anything or anyone that is unreasonable or prevents us from doing our job. No disrespect, but as photographers, we have found that Episcopal churches are by far the most strict with regards to photography.

I'm no stranger to religious oppression. I was raised Southern Baptist. As a child I was told that dancing is a sin and rock n' roll music will literally melt your brain before you end up burning in the fiery bowels of hell (say that last part with a dramatic Southern drawl and you get where I'm coming from). So now that I'm all grown up, I get a perverse satisfaction from wearing a T-shirt I bought at a Southern Culture on the Skids concert under my conservative suit and tie at Baptist weddings.

You know what we won't go to hell for at a Baptist wedding? They don't mind if we photograph the ceremony! Wow, imagine that. It's fine as long as we observe a three-page list of rules, but we still get to be inside the sanctuary and photograph the event. It's the same with Methodists, Catholics, and Presbyterians and even in most synagogues.

Most Episcopal churches, on the other hand, don't allow us to photograph the ceremony at all. Some actually assign people to sit with us outside the sanctuary to be sure that we don't try to sneak a photo. We can hear everything going on, we're just not allowed to peek inside. I'm not sure what they're afraid of; I paid the extra hundred bucks for the camera that doesn't steal your soul. It just seems like a lost opportunity.

It's not all bad, though. A few of these churches are super progressive and allow one, yes, you read that correctly, **one** image to be created during the entire ceremony. On one occasion, I remember the moment I stepped into the sanctuary before a wedding, the church lady cheerfully reminded me, "Now remember, you only get to take one picture, so choose wisely." She even shook her finger in that way that said, "I'm acting friendly now, but if you cross me, I will gut you like a hog."

I'll let you in on a little secret. If you ever marry in an Episcopal church, plan to have a lot of music spaced evenly throughout the ceremony. Loud organ solos, or perhaps a vocalist who can fill the room with her voice. While the music is playing,

I'll be shooting like crazy and getting the results you paid me to get. You didn't hear that from me though.

Sir Sux-a-Lot—This is a DJ or Emcee who doesn't do a good job of reading the crowd and, as a result, can't keep the party going. Even with our advanced photo technology, it's hard to capture people having fun when they're not actually having fun. There's just no Photoshop filter for that. People think that DJs have an easy job. They just play some songs from a list and make a few announcements, right? A bad DJ can deep-six a party in less time than it takes to finish the Casper Slide Parts 1 and 2. Too many lame tunes in a set and the next thing you know, your friends are down the street at a bar watching the game instead of watching you cut a cake.

Sir Sux-a-Lot is usually a great guy, and he's helpful too. He'll make an announcement after dinner that all of the guests should come to the dance floor because "The photographer wants to take a big group photo." The first time that happened to me I was floored and completely confused. I thought: "This wasn't discussed. Was it a request from the bride that I didn't know about? He didn't even ask me if I was ready to do something like that. How am I going to get a shot with that many people? What the hell, man?" It turned out that the

DJ didn't care if I was going to take a photo or not. It was just his ploy to get as many people on the dance floor as possible. Later that night, Jimmy may or may not have let the air out of his tires.

Eleanor Rigby—The church lady who has her eye on us to make sure we don't color outside the lines or break any of the three pages of church rules. Not quite as severe as an Episcopalian, Eleanor is a more polite enforcer. Among church ladies, there seems to be a universal culture of distrust when it comes to photographers. They have a mental archive full of horror stories about photographers who acted unprofessionally or disrupted the ceremony. And it's Eleanor's mission to never let that happen again.

When I first walk into the church and introduce myself, a casual interrogation ensues that goes something like this:

> **Eleanor:** So have you been here before?
>
> **Me:** Yes I have. My wife and I were here just a few months ago.
>
> **Eleanor:** Great. So you know the rules?
>
> **Me:** Sure. No flash, no crossing the threshold into the sanctuary after the bride is in, I have to stay in the bal-

cony, and no moving around during the ceremony.

Eleanor: That's right. The photographer last week disregarded everything. Walked up the aisle just clicking away and being quite disruptive. I thought I was going to die. I swore I'd make sure he never worked here again.

Me: I can assure you we will be discreet.

Eleanor: Good, and remember that you only have twenty minutes total for family pictures in the sanctuary once all the guests are out.

Sometimes we do have to bend the rules a little to get that perfect shot. At the end of the day though, it's worth it because you trade three minutes of abuse from Eleanor for some great images that will be with your clients forever. Besides, we're already in church, so we just ask forgiveness and move on.

Matlock Posse—Named after the Matlock TV show from the 1980s. This is the group of guys, usually the groom's frat brothers, who show up in seersucker suits and colorful bow ties (just like Andy Griffith's Matlock character wore on the show). These guys have uppity first names like Bryce or Hamilton, and they are nearly always single because, seriously, whose wife is going to let them out of the house like that?

Living and working in the South, we do a lot of coastal weddings, and you can always count on seeing a Matlock Posse. The weird part is that you'd think the style would evolve a little over the years. Nope. It's always a standard-issue seersucker suit, white or pink shirt, pastel bow tie with tiny embroidered sailfish or anchors, and deck shoes (sans socks, of course).

Single females should always be on the lookout for members of this notorious group. He may look like he's ready to go hunt Easter eggs, but that's just a disguise to throw you off. For once a member of the posse identifies a woman as "available," he will go to extraordinary lengths to win her over. His goal is to keep a fresh drink in her hand at all times, and after a celebratory evening of grinding out on the dance floor, he'll create a distraction so her friends don't notice the "new couple" headed back to his hotel.

Chapter 2
The Quest for Beauty and Comfort

Most unmarried men have no clue what women go through to look and feel their best on any given day. You can multiply that effort by ten on a woman's wedding day. While most grooms are kicking back and having a few drinks before the ceremony, the bride has a strict schedule that involves a team of beauty experts at multiple locations, plus several layers of garments, hooks, and infrastructure that must all work together. Keeping that dress on, the hair back, and the "girls" up yet not exposed requires creativity and unorthodox techniques.

Ninety-eight percent of our brides have never been married before and have never gone through this level of preparation to look "more beautiful than ever." The magazines tell them to wear more makeup than usual to enhance their features and look better in photos. The hairdresser insists that hair should be pulled back and put up into an elaborately constructed bun, which takes an hour to create and is immediately covered by a veil. I imagine that a bride becomes overwhelmed, torn between what the people around her say is "the norm for this kind of thing" while trying to retain a shred of her own personal style. Some go too far when making the transformation from everyday hair and makeup to wedding day glam; others don't go far enough and may as well be wearing a ponytail with that fabulous ball gown.

When it comes to hair, makeup, and bridal fashion there is a line that is not to be crossed. While the line is different for everyone, it's important to remember that this is a wedding, not a pageant for drag queens (in most cases). Because most brides lack experience in getting married, it's sometimes not obvious to them when the line has been crossed from gorgeous to a less desirable Nicki-Minaj-style freak show. The only solution is to hire professional hair and makeup people (the kind that specialize in weddings, not drag shows).

Looking good on the big day is one thing, but feeling good is also on the must-have list. The goal isn't always physical comfort. Prewedding jitters, butterflies, and sheer terror can make a girl want to hit the bottle and hide in the closet. There's also that sinking question in the pit of her stomach: what if this marriage doesn't work out in the long run and Daddy will be pissed for having spent a chunk of his retirement fund on the wedding? No matter what you call it, emotional comfort is just as important to some folks as physical comfort. Knowing that they are about to be put on display in front of hundreds of people with at least a few dozen of those being judgmental in-laws and sorority sisters is enough to leave a girl balled up in the corner babbling to herself. This need for calm and composure can extend beyond the bride to the groom, the parents, and the rest of the wedding party. The solutions to their anxiety issues make for some interesting situations. Alcohol, drugs, chiropractors, therapists, and hypnotists—nothing is off the table in the quest for emotional comfort and calming irrational fears.

You Won't See This Tip In Ms. Stewart's Magazine

One thing I have learned over the years is that when given the choice, most women preparing to be the center of attention for an entire day would rather be beautiful than comfortable. They are willing to endure pain for eight to ten hours in a gorgeous pair of four-inch Jimmy Choos simply because they look fabulous in them. Even if the reality is that few people if any will ever catch a glimpse of them under the dress. Likewise, they might tell themselves that the half-hour of uncontrollable tears brought on by the glue from applying false eyelashes is a small price to pay for looking your very best.

If you've never been behind the scenes at a wedding, then you have no idea the great lengths brides go to look and feel beautiful on their wedding day. The rooms where the ladies get ready can look like a special-effects workshop with all of the tools and chemicals for the hair and makeup regimes. When a makeup artist walks in the room with three rolling cases of products for air brushing the skin to a buttery smooth texture, you have to wonder if she has hideous subjects to transform or if she's just over prepared. It's the latter more often than not. Don't think for a minute that I'm complaining, though. The better my subjects look, the better my resulting photos. My job will be easier later when I'm retouching the images. So by all means, I am supportive of taking as much time as needed to get their pretty on.

The hair and makeup are complex enough; then there is the structural engineering that goes into the dress. As expensive as a wedding dress is and as much custom fitting and alterations that happen along the way, you would think it should fit perfectly. That perfect fit does happen, but it's more the exception than the rule. I'm not pointing the blame for that at anyone in particular, but I suggest that once a bride has been to her final dress fitting, it might be a good time to stop trying to lose those last five pounds. It will affect the way the dress fits. Sewing, taping, and ripping underlining to achieve just the right fit in all the right places just hours before walking down the aisle is a tension-filled scramble that can set the tone for the remainder of the day.

When it happens, the scenario involves the bride barking orders, bridesmaids trying to keep her calm, and a mother who is paralyzed with worry that she will make a wrong move and get yelled at for ruining everything. Oh, and now the dress won't zip all the way up, and she suddenly regrets those two bites of cheesecake she enjoyed at the rehearsal dinner last night.

For a guy like me, this all seems a little over the top, which is why I have devised a fantastic plan to avoid all of the getting-ready drama. I simply have my wife, Meridith, cover the photography for all of the women getting ready, and I work with the guys. With that master plan in place, there is a lot that goes on in the ladies' dressing room that I get to skip, and I'm very okay with that.

One fine wedding day we were working in Asheville, North Carolina. Everything was going along perfectly. Every wedding season, we get that one event that we just know is going to be our "wedding of the year," the one where all of the right visual elements come together to land you that sought-after eight-page real-wedding feature in a national magazine. For us, this was it.

The ceremony took place in the very proper English-style garden of a castle-like manor built in the early 1920s. A thick blanket of pink rose petals covered the lawn on either side of the aisle leading up to a stone gazebo, where the vows would be exchanged. Roses and tulips were in full bloom all around us, filling the scene with bold colors and subtle textures straight out of an impressionist painting. The bride and groom were both photogenic, affectionate toward each other, and took direction easily. For a photographer, it just doesn't get much better than that. All of the hard work and effort that the wedding planner put into this had come together flawlessly.

The ceremony happened just as it was scripted and Emily and Steve were five minutes into being a happily married couple when I began setting up for the family group photos. I could tell that Emily was pleased by the way she was looking around at everything and taking in all of the scenery. It was the fairy-tale scene she had dreamed about.

As usual after a ceremony, the families were gathered around in the garden waiting for photos to begin. Everyone was laughing and congratulating the couple, telling Emily how great she looked, and recounting the cute little quirky things that happened during the ceremony—like how she messed up part of her vows and he had trouble getting the ring on her finger. I let them all chat and went about setting up my light, getting my camera settings locked in, and trying to gauge just how many people would be in the first group photo. Out of the corner of my eye, I saw Emily drop something. I automatically assumed it was her handkerchief. It's typical for brides to carry a sentimental handkerchief decked out with embroidery and their wedding date or monogram. They often wrap them around the stems of their bouquet and just as often drop them when hugging people or changing their flowers from one hand to the other. Emily was busy chatting, so without much thought, I leaned down to pick up the hanky. It was then that I actually took a look at what I was about to pick up.

You know how in certain situations in life, like train wrecks and car crashes, everything moves in slow motion, and it seems like you have time for a million thoughts to run through your mind in the blink of an eye? That's exactly what happened to me. As I was leaning toward the handkerchief, the whole world around me slowed to nearly a stop. I developed tunnel vision and began a conversation in my brain:

"Oh wow, that's not a hanky at all. Whoa, wait, what is that? I've seen something like that before, but where? Holy crap that's a freakin' maxi pad! What the hell is a maxi pad doing here? OMG that just fell out from under her dress! I'm pretty sure that's gross, but how is it even possible? Why am I still reaching for it? *Must abort mission*! Is anyone watching me do this? How did this happen? This is so awkward. Okay, how can I play it off? Do I just stand back up? Do I try to kick it aside? I'll just act like nothing happened. What if she freaks out? Someone's going to notice eventually, that thing is huge…Oh, shit! Another one just fell out of her dress. *What is happening?*"

It felt like those two seconds took years off of my life and with all of the finesse I could muster, I stood back up as casually as possible and tried to play it off by going about my business of setting up the group shots, as if I saw nothing. I am certain that it looked like some lame-ass attempt at a modern dance move, but luckily, because everyone was so busy talking to each other, I don't think that anyone really saw what almost happened or the abandoned pads laying in the rose-petal-laden aisle. (They had wings y'all.)

In a mild state of shock, I had another internal conversation with myself, which involved lots of follow-up questions: Why did that just happen? How is it physically possible that it could happen? How has no one noticed yet? Am I on a hidden camera TV show? Will Emily freak when she realizes? Seriously, how in the hell did that happen? Most important, what will it take to wipe this perplexed look off of my face?

Now with my own personal disaster averted, I wasn't out of the woods yet. We still had to take the family photos where the two unfortunate items were laying on the ground. Surprised that no one had done anything, I played through in my mind things to make the problem go away. Maybe I could just make the photos with them still on the ground then retouch them, like nothing ever happened. I could ask everyone to move a few steps toward me so they would be standing on top of them. Better yet, I could ask someone to slap me and wake me from this weirdo dream I was having. By the time it became necessary to address the problem, Emily finally noticed her discarded unmentionables and casually whispered to Steve to pick them up and put them in his jacket pocket, which he did without a second thought or hesitation, as if that happened all the time. Neither seemed the least bit mortified, which had me wondering if I was the crazy one.

Once the family photos were complete, I rushed over to Meridith and asked if there was any good reason why maxi pads would be falling from under the bride's dress in the middle of the garden and no one notice. I expected an expression of shock and surprise.

She just shrugged and said, "Oh yeah, they put pads under her dress," as if it was a totally normal thing.

I began to realize that I was the one going nuts and the only one who found this out of the ordinary.

"Why the hell would they do that?" I asked.

Meridith explained in a matter-of-fact way that earlier that afternoon, when Emily put on her dress, the built-in corset was fitting extra tight, and the stiff supports were digging into her skin. That made simple tasks like walking and breathing quite uncomfortable for her. One of her bridesmaids got the bright idea to place a few pads between the dress and her skin around Emily's waist and rib cage. I guess by the time the ceremony was over, the adhesive had succumbed to the heat and perspiration. Since Meridith was a witness to that part of the day, it made total sense to her.

"A girl's got to do whatever is necessary to rock that dress," she said.

I received no sympathy from her for my trauma.

The rest of the day was drama-free and filled with fantastic photo opportunities. I have to hand it to our bride: *A*-plus for improvisation. But a ten out of ten on the awkward scale for me. I learned so much in those couple of seconds and now I look more closely at every situation before jumping into action. You just never know what's under that dress.

Most Memorable Quotes Ever

"Okay, girls: booger check."

A bride to her attendants just before
walking down the aisle.

Out to Lunch

A wedding day is a big deal for everyone involved. So much time and effort has gone into who will be invited, how everything will look, and who will sit together at the reception. A significant amount of money has been spent to feed and entertain the guests. It's understandable that brides and their families are nervous about living up to all the expectations, the social interactions, and being on display in front of so many people. Everyone gets a little nervous when they have to perform, but overcompensating is one sure way to get your story told here.

Candice was a quiet Southern belle and just as sweet as could be. We arrived at her ceremony location confident that the wedding day would be a slam-dunk. It was a beautiful spring day. The birds were singing, the flowers were blooming, and puffy white clouds were lazily drifting through the sky. Everything was set for a garden wedding, and we were fully energized and ready to make some great images. We had a fun-loving couple, and both the ceremony and the reception were at the same location, which makes everyone's lives so much easier. What could go wrong?

Of course, it's never *that* easy is it?

When we got out of the car, we saw that Candice had just pulled up and parked few spaces away. She got out, said hello, gave me a big hug, and told us that she was headed to her room to get ready. I noticed that she seemed a little, let's call it starry-eyed, but I didn't think much of it. Brides always have about seven hundred things going through their mind the day of their wedding.

Meridith and I parted ways so she could follow Candice, and I went about shooting details and scene-setting images of the gardens and plantation house. About a half-hour later, Meridith came out of the room where the ladies were getting ready and said that Candice was not in the best of shape. She had been super nervous all day and had just taken her third Xanax a few moments ago.

"Okay," I said. "What's Xanax, and why is that a big deal?" So I looked it up on my phone. Our girl Candice had taken a strong antianxiety medication. She was about five feet tall with heels on and maybe ninety-two pounds. I was not sure if that stuff works by weight the way alcohol does, but either way it looked like she was well over the recommended dose. The worst part was that it wasn't even her prescription. Meridith said that as Candice was getting ready, she became increasingly distant and was getting to the point of incoherence. Like in the cartoons when shades are pulled down over the character's eyes that say "out to lunch."

We hadn't even started taking pictures of her yet! How were we going to work this? Most guests wouldn't know that we photographers are on the job several hours before the ceremony happens to document the bride and groom as they get ready separately. Then we attempt to create as many group photos of family and friends as time permits before the ceremony. Based on my phone call with Candice the week before, we were supposed to be taking her and her bridesmaids into the garden for photos before the guests arrived. The only problem was, she was on the sofa staring into space and wasn't moving. Everyone else in the room was quietly going about their makeup routines and trying their best to pretend that Candice was just fine.

With Candice sitting catatonic on the sofa, there wasn't much happening in the bridal suite, so Meridith and I ducked out to get some fresh air and revise our strategy for how to salvage the day. I decided that we would not limit the amount of photos we made; we would simply change what we pointed our camera at. Instead of pictures of the bride, we would spend our time creating beautiful pictures of scenery and everyone else until this Xanax stuff wore off.

When we returned to the room, Candice was sitting exactly where we left her, but now she had on her dress. I looked at Meridith with an expression that said, "How did that happen?" I hoped that since she had obviously moved recently, maybe the drug was wearing off and we could begin photos. But she was still staring out the window and not speaking. Feeling pressure to make something out of this situation, I asked if I could take a few photos of her as she sat on the sofa. Without looking my direction, she nodded yes. She couldn't focus on one thing for any length of time. It was useless to attempt making images of her looking at the camera. So I used dramatic lighting and photographed her in dreamy far off glances looking in any direction but the camera's. I'm sure she was having an out of body experience; she was the calmest person I have ever seen who was not either dead or asleep. I was really interested to see how the ceremony was going to play out. It was only an hour away and this poor girl was in no shape for it.

Most wedding-day stress that we experience comes from deviating from the previously agreed upon plan. Switching to plan B is one thing, but we were way beyond that now. Candice and I had discussed the wedding-day schedule in detail the week before, and her pharmaceutical vacation was throwing everything off. But there is a fix to just about any problem. This woman paid me to create great photos of her wedding, so I was determined to make something out of this situation. "How do I work this?" I thought to myself. Pacing in the hallway trying to come up with a good solution, I was also imagining the conversation with Candice a few weeks later:

> **Candice:** I love the faraway pictures you did, but gosh, I look spaced out in every picture you took.
> **Me:** You seemed very relaxed. Was everything okay that day?
> **Candice:** Of course! I was fine. I remember everything. You were there, people were there; there were unicorns, and leprechauns, and lots of pretty fairies. It was wonderful! Now, can you fix my face in all of these pictures?

Candice still wasn't talking much, and her friend who supplied the pills was freaking out thinking that she had ruined the wedding by drugging the bride. It was twenty minutes till go time when Candice's bridesmaids realized that they had a big problem. They jumped into action and began talking loudly and forcing her to drink as much diet soda as they could to wake the girl up.

Meridith and I left Candice as the bridesmaids huddled around trying to bring her back to coherence. We made our way out to the garden to photograph guests arriving, programs being handed out, and to cover the musicians. The area was bustling with activity as people were seated and lively conversations ensued between friends and family, some of whom had not seen each other in years. As I scanned the crowd looking to capture animated folks and their expressions, I couldn't stop thinking about how not one of these people had a clue as to what was going on upstairs in the manor house.

"They have no idea that they will probably be sitting here for a very long time, if this thing even happens at all," I muttered under my breath.

I expected that it would take at least another hour or more of bridesmaids pumping her full of caffeine and yelling, "Okay, Shug, you can do this." Even if they get her back on her feet, they would need two people to drag her down the aisle. I wondered how legit a wedding is when you say your vows in such a state of mind. Checking my watch, I was relieved that things were only five minutes behind schedule so far. But in about five more minutes, the nosier members of the audience would get restless and begin seeking out anyone who looked like they might be in charge to ask what was going on.

It was half-past five when I checked the time again. The string trio was to begin playing about fifteen minutes before Candice hit the aisle, and they had some lovely material to fill that time frame. Forty-five minutes later there was still no bride. I began to recognize that the musicians were repeating songs and had played a few three times already. They kept looking at each other with expressions of "How in the hell much longer?"

Eventually, a few of the groomsmen nudged each other and nodded in the direction of the manor house, I knew something was happening. I looked around the corner and saw Candice emerging from the front entrance accompanied by her father.

I was happy but surprised. I guess adrenaline and butterflies balanced out the drug's effects. Candice finally had it together at last and was able to walk again, smile again, and even look at you without looking through you. Score! She was back to about 80 percent of her normal demeanor, which was good enough for none of the guests to notice. I'm not even sure that her groom, William, knew what was going on. Standing holding hands underneath a huge oak tree, Candice swayed back and forth a little during the ceremony. Anyone out in the audience would have thought that she was either nervous or trying to get the sun out of her eyes. I kept waiting for her to drop. But to my astonishment, she got through the whole thing without incident.

I learned later that Xanax relaxes you and lowers your breathing rate. It doesn't make you see unicorns or leprechauns unless they are actually there with you. Too much causes drowsiness, dizziness, confusion, and shortness of breath. It also causes your expressions to look completely whack when trying to smile for a camera. So please follow directions carefully!

Keeping the Girls in Line

This fashion tip comes straight from one of our brides who is a former Miss America contestant. Along with the sparkly gowns, being on TV in a bikini, and getting to meet the guy who sings: "Here She Comes" or "There She Is" or whatever that famous song is, it sounds like you also pick up unique beauty and fashion tips in the pageant world.

When we walked into the suite where the bridal party was getting ready, we had no idea that Anna was a former beauty queen. All we knew was that she was currently a medical student. As she began to photograph Anna, Meridith noticed that she was doing her own makeup and was good at it. Applying makeup is one of those things that we have found to be optional for many medical students, who in most cases feel that they have more pressing things to worry about.

Through casual conversation and much to our embarrassment, we learned that Anna was a former Miss North Carolina and had placed well in the Miss America Pageant just a few months before.

As she finished her makeup and prepared to leave for the church, she yelled to her sister, "Don't forget to throw the duct tape in my bag."

We learned so much from Anna that day. For example, if you want to flaunt great looking cleavage, skip Victoria's Secret and shop at Home Depot.

In the course of searching for all of the things one might need to look and feel fabulous on her wedding day, many brides neglect to put a ton of thought into their foundational undergarment situation. Either the support is built into the top of the dress, or it isn't. But why not create your own completely customizable cleavage for a fraction of the cost department stores charge? It can be done, and we have Anna to thank for it.

Simply head down to your local hardware store and get yourself a roll of duct tape. That's right, I said duct tape, the magical, silvery grayish, super sticky stuff that manly men use to fix just about everything. If you look in the right place, you'll find that they even make it in fancy colors. Now I worked as a photographer in the advertising industry for ten years before I worked with weddings. I shot a lot of fashion, including lingerie, and I thought I had seen all the tricks of the trade to attain just the right amount of cleavage.

There is no shortage of products on the market, including pads, inserts, and things that look like chicken cutlets, to help fill out, push up, and generally create something from nothing to get you noticed. It turns out that this little-discussed technique of taping your chest has been used in the pageant world for decades. But Meridith and I had never seen such a radical yet practical technique used at a wedding until we met Anna.

So we're clear, it's not lost on me that this might seem just a tiny bit extreme to some folks. Why not just get the right bra and be done? You might wonder how sexy is it to start off your honeymoon night by ducking into the bathroom and ripping a strong adhesive strip from sensitive places. If you ever consider doing this, you will no doubt have some questions. Do you remove slowly, or fast? Then you're thinking, "Will my skin come off with it? Crap! I've never done this before! Well, here goes. Damn, this stuff is strong! Not as bad as waxing, but man, how long is this big ass, red stripe going to be there, and how do I remove this adhesive residue?"

Then, the lights get low and your still slightly intoxicated husband gets romantic all of a sudden. When he snuggles in close, the first thing that comes to his mind shouldn't be, "Hey, something here is familiar. It's not perfume, but this kind of reminds me of how my toolbox smells. Why does the skin on her boobs feel like the back of a Post-it note?"

So while a simple off-the-shelf bra may have been the easy way to go, to those of you doubters I can only say, "Beauty ain't always pretty."

While we didn't exactly see the tape being applied, the technique was quite the topic of discussion among the bridesmaids. Since Anna was using this method herself on her own wedding day, we knew there must be something to it. The procedure itself is pretty simple, but it might require a little practice in terms of exact placement. First, pull enough tape off the roll to go from under one arm to under the other. When in doubt, it's best to have too much rather than not enough, especially if you tend to sweat a lot. Tack one end of the tape gently on one side of your chest just below where the top of the dress' bodice falls. The placement should not be straight across the chest but rather just under for support and the "push-up factor."

The tricky part is deciding how much cleavage to create before tacking down the other end of the tape. You want to make sure the cleavage is centered, and, of course, depending on how much cleavage you need to hold together, you may need another piece of tape. I considered including a diagram, but that would mean this book would be organized with the bondage and alternative-lifestyle books.

Nothing is Real

Some days I'm a makeup artist, other days I'm a personal trainer. When necessary, I become a full-service plastic surgeon. It's commonplace for me to give clients a jaw line or a chin. Maybe I smooth out that little bump on the bridge of the nose, or take a few pounds off of each arm. I do all of this without a license or any surgical credentials and from the comfort of a cushy office chair. Most clients don't know that I did work on them, but they certainly notice if I don't. Women are brutal when it comes to looking at photos of themselves. They can pick out every possible flaw, so it's my job to stay one step ahead.

The bottom line is that photos you have seen in magazines and advertisements are completely worked over, beating out every conceivable bit of reality. You probably knew that already, but you should also apply the same standard to your friends' wedding album or their family Christmas card. Never believe anything you see in photos. It's all a lie, and that's the truth.

I've overheard many of our brides discussing the crash diets they endure to lose the extra fifteen or twenty pounds that stand between feeling confident wearing their dress and hating the way they look. The all-juice diet comes to mind. "I just stopped eating for a few weeks" is another favorite method. The lengths that some women go to reach their ideal weight are admirable. They could no doubt move mountains if they applied the same focus and intensity to other areas of their lives.

My only advice is to be careful what you wish for. Being fit and healthy is great, but that's not what we're talking about here. When a bride is focused on getting skinny to look good in a dress, it has nothing to do with being fit or healthy. She just wants to look good as quickly as possible.

You might be thinking, Awe, that's so sweet, James wants his clients to be happy and healthy. What I'm really thinking about is how a bride slimming down quickly is going to cause me do a lot of retouching to her armpits. Yeah, you read that right.

I should probably explain. Dainty arms are great. What woman wouldn't want them? But what happens to all that skin after the fat underneath melts away? It gets all wrinkly and gross. It's not just you, though. Models have it as bad as anyone. I know this because I still photograph a good bit of fashion for wedding magazines, and those women are skinny. Like call-911-and-order-them-a-double-cheeseburger-with-fries skinny.

One fall when I was super busy with a hundred other projects, I was in the office working hard to get images edited and out to the publisher for a wedding gown fashion shoot that I did a few weeks earlier. I was a few days past deadline for delivering the files, so I buckled down and told myself I wouldn't get up from my desk until the photos were on their way to the magazine. I anticipated that this would take about two hours. While it's true that a lot of retouching goes into every image you see in a magazine, it's also true that most of the time the models are attractive already and the talents of the makeup artist transforms them to stunning. There is always some smoothing and blending to be done in postproduction but nothing that is time consuming.

I was prepping twenty-one images that would each be printed full page in the magazine. The photos looked good and the retouching was going well until I zoomed in and noticed that the skin on one of the model's arms needed major smoothing. Her arms were toned, she had a great body, and her face was gorgeous, but the area around her armpit looked withered and needed something to plump it out. When the light hit a certain way, her wrinkled pit skin created texture and shadows that needed a great deal of smoothing and blending. This girl was in nearly half of the images, so I knew then that my plans for the rest of the day were shot.

A few hours into fixing this issue, my mood was going from annoyed to pissed and then all the way to numb and defeated. That's when my phone buzzed. It was a text message from Robyn, the publisher, politely asking if the fashion images were ready. Her graphic designer was hot to get them into the layout. The following text conversation actually happened:

> **Robyn:** Is Fashion Ready? Need to get pics to Steph for layout.
>
> **James:** Going slow, I didn't notice at the shoot, but this girl's armpits.
>
> **Robyn:** Armpits?
>
> **James:** Yeah, won't say what they look like cause it's rude, but it's taking a lot of work to fix.
>
> **Robyn:** You know I don't care about rude, what's it look like?

James: An old wrinkly elephant vagina. (Screen photo attached)
Robyn: OMG! It does! Eeeeewww!
James: I can't un-see this.
Robyn: Hahaha! Go look at a Vogue and stare at those models.

Some images were easier to fix than others depending on her arm placement. For example, if she had her hands on her hips, all of that skin around her pits was stretched out and looked smoother already. If she had her arms by her side it was rough. Each image took an additional fifteen to thirty minutes to smooth and blend the skin, taking it from "old wrinkly elephant vagina" to what I imagine you might see on a much younger elephant. Several hours later I emerged victorious, and the doctors say that I should be fine after a few more rounds of electro-shock therapy.

Most Memorable Quotes Ever

"I don't have pockets. Who can carry this tampon for me?"

Bride shouting to her bridesmaids
just before the ceremony.

Corpse Bride

A lot of people think that because I'm a wedding photographer, I only work on Saturdays. That would be great if it were true. During the week, I am busy photographing other types of sessions that relate to a wedding. It might be a couple's engagement session, where we go out to a location that is special to them and create casual portraits. In the South, a bride's mother will often commission a formal bridal portrait. That is a session where we photograph the bride in her gown several weeks before the wedding. The goal is to put the framed portrait on display at the reception for all of the guests to see. If you are not from the South, you may be asking, Why would they put up a picture of the bride when the real girl is standing in the same room wearing the same dress? That is a perfectly normal reaction for un-Southerners.

It would be nice to think that if you hire a competent photographer for an engagement or bridal portrait all you need to do is show up. Well, things just don't work that way. It's important for clients to bring their A-game to the photo shoot too. Frizzy hair, inappropriate clothing, a groom with the personality of a small soap dish are all things that will be noticed in the resulting photos no matter how great my lighting, composition, or backgrounds might appear in the image.

It is also a major part of my job to put each person I photograph at ease, keep them comfortable, and bring out the best in them during their photo shoot. If you look at a gorgeous photo but the expressions of the people in it seem off, that's because the photographer pushed them past their comfort zone and into their awkward zone. Often the first three minutes of a session can make the difference between amazing, average, or grueling. Grueling is to be avoided at all costs.

I was scheduled for Robin's bridal session on a September day in downtown Raleigh. She and her mom requested the location to be their church. It's unusual for me to do a bridal session at the church since we'll be back there a few weeks later for the actual wedding. I prefer sessions at a more neutral location with a greater variety of scenery, like a garden or downtown area. I'm all for keeping people happy though, so I made my way to their church ready to create something awesome.

I was told to meet Robin and her mom inside the building behind the sanctuary, where all of the classrooms and offices are located. When I arrived, I found that the door was unlocked, so I walked in expecting so see someone. It appeared that I was the only one around. I assumed they were running late, as appointments often do, but then I heard a loud noise down the hallway. Walking in a little farther, I asked myself, What did I just hear? I thought I was the only one here, but I guess not. As I walked down the hall, what I was hearing was actually yelling. Not the "Praise the Lord!" kind of yelling you might expect to hear in a Southern church. These were furious, gut-wrenching screams coming from a place of deep emotional distress. At first I thought someone was in trouble, so I quickly made my way toward the sound. As I got closer, I realized it was Robin screaming at her mom.

"Look at my makeup! For the love of God, Mother, I look like death! I'm a *corpse bride!*"

I stood outside in the hallway, eyes bugging out of my head in shock. Did I really just hear that? I kept looking around for the hidden camera that was surely filming me for the joke. In the span of ten minutes I stood in the hall and heard that same line screamed at least a dozen times.

"What do I do? *I look like death!*" she would scream. I could tell that her mom was trying to calm her down, but Robin was in no mood for calm.

I was about ready to pack it up and go home. Even though I had yet to see or speak with anyone, I was sure this session was going nowhere. I could create beautiful imagery that would bring tears to your eyes, but if the girl doesn't like her makeup, it's game over. I called Meridith and told her what was going on, as if she could council me on what to say to Robin. Of course, there is no tech-support hotline for brides melting down, so she wished me luck. I went back to pacing.

The session was about thirty minutes behind. No one had emerged from the room yet. Things had gotten quiet, but there was no way I was going to go knock on the door. I moved down the hall and around the corner so that when they did come out it would be easier to pretend that I didn't hear anything. Eventually, Robin emerged and greeted me pleasantly, as if her melt down never happened. I tried to play it off by saying that I just arrived. But I'm a bad liar, and I imagine that I looked like a deer in headlights.

For the record, I thought Robin's makeup looked fine. Having met her several times before, I knew she was an accountant and recalled that her everyday makeup regime was conservative.

Sometimes brides do get a little freaked out when they see themselves glammed up, as if no one else will recognize them. While she was not exactly tan and her eye makeup was heavier than usual, I wasn't getting any goth-chick vibes from her look. The biggest thing against her was that the room she was in had horrific fluorescent lights, which can make any fresh-faced fifteen year old look sixty-two. One glance into that mirror and most anyone would have thought they looked like death. Robin seemed calm now, but I proceeded with the session as if I was disarming a bomb.

Once we began, I kept Robin calm by using soothing, positive words. I walked on eggshells for the whole thing, thinking her Dr. Jekyll would go Mr. Hyde on me any second. About halfway through the session, I realized that she was fine. She apparently had her freak-out, accepted her situation, and was okay now. I also got the clear sense that I was working with a mom who wanted everything to be perfect for her little girl and a daughter who was used to attention but could snap at any moment to get more attention.

I walked away feeling I had wasted my time, but the images turned out beautifully. Sometimes it's the smallest things that a woman doesn't like about her appearance, especially makeup or hair, that can make her dislike a photograph. Surprise and relief came a few weeks later when I heard how happy they were with the images. They ordered several to put on display at the reception, so I knew they weren't just playing along.

We never spoke of the makeup incident, and both Robin and her mom were the nicest clients I could hope for. The wedding a few weeks later was buttery smooth with no screaming, though the makeup was a little different. It just goes to show that you can't judge every session by the first three minutes.

Behind the Scenes Insight

Most of the clients we work with have never been married and have no idea what to expect. While many of them have attended other weddings, that experience only offers a general idea of how things work, which can instill a false sense of confidence. Even though neither the bride nor the groom have been in this role before, it's funny to us how they still expect everything to go perfectly. We created this list of things that are more the rule than the exception. So if you are a bride to be, here is your list of...

James D. Walters

Thirteen Things That Are More Common than You Might Think

1. You will be on your period on the wedding day. Nature is cruel and runs on its own schedule. Even though you accounted for this monthly inconvenience when choosing the date, the months go by, stress and dieting take their toll on the body, and hours before walking down the aisle you find yourself sending your maid of honor to the store for a box of super-absorbent something-or-others. How do I know this? In the times when I am around the ladies as they are get-ting ready, they'll either forget I'm there or figure that I have seen and heard it all before. Next thing you know I'm one of the girls, and they're talking about all sorts of stuff I would be happy to forget if I could.

2. The limo driver will ask for direc-tions. The newly married couple runs through the crowd of well-wishers and are ushered into a gorgeous 1950s Bentley. The driver turns around and says, "Congratulations, you guys. Where are we headed?" That's if the driver arrives on time, or at all. Nothing against limo companies, but I've seen this scenario play out so often that I once started a wedding-car company of my own.

3. The presider will either forget your new name or mispronounce it. There's that moment at the end of every ceremony where the presider (priest, minister, Preacher-man) says a little prayer and then delivers the big introduction of Mr. and Mrs. Whomever. The audience stands and cheers, and it's a great moment. It's also the time that many presiders, caught up in the excitement, completely obliterate the pronunciation of the groom's last name. It's both hysterical and mortifying. The crowd gets a good laugh, and by this time the couple is facing their guests. So when they hear the mispronunciation, they look at each other with an expression that says, "Well, he completely effed up our name, but I guess we're married anyway, so let's walk up this aisle together!"

4. The band will repeatedly mispronounce someone's name. It happens with bands just as often as presiders. First names, last names—bands can be equal opportunity name garblers. But it's way more entertaining to see what happens next. Call the bride or groom the wrong thing, and it's a good bet that someone in the band will have an overexcited bridesmaid spitting the correct name in his or her ear in whatever time it takes for her to stumble up to the stage. It's even funnier when after a few slip ups, the whole crowd becomes irate and begins shouting in unison at the band. At a reception we covered in Charlotte, the bandleader kept calling the groom *Jason*. His name was *Justin*, and even after being corrected a few times, the bandleader still invited "Jason to escort his mother to the dance floor for the mother-son dance." That's all it took. The next thing I saw was the maid of honor up in this guy's grill shaking a finger. Later on we saw a big sign taped to the band leader's microphone stand scribbled in bold marker that read: "It's Justin!"

5. At least one groomsman will forget to bring socks. I wish someone could explain why this happens, but being a guy, I already know why. As a general rule, our gender might not be best at thinking ahead and planning. When a groomsman shows up to the hotel in flip-flops and his sights are set on scoring with that cute red headed bridesmaid he flirted with at the rehearsal dinner, I guess I can see where socks might not have crossed his mind. For groomsmen, nearly everything they wear aside from their skivvies comes in the bag that they picked up from the tuxedo shop. They assume it's all there, from the tie to the shoes, and are stunned to learn that they need to supply their own black socks! "Where am I gonna find socks?" This starts a frantic series of calls to the other groomsmen and eventually the crisis is averted. Of course this all goes down within an hour before you walk down the aisle, so be glad that you don't know about everything that happens that day.

6. None of the groomsmen will know how cufflinks work. I know it sounds like I'm picking on the guys, but it's comical to see grown men defeated by small fashion accessories. When first removed from the package, the cuff links get a cursory and somewhat puzzled inspection. The expression on the guy's face shows that this is uncharted water for him. He scans the room for an older and wiser chap to guide him through the process. Then there is the confident but equally clueless groomsman who forges ahead and either puts them in completely backward or, even better, rolls the cuff while everyone else has theirs French style. Call me a snob, but come on, guys, a little style up in here!

7. You will need to be sewn into or cut out of your dress. You may have bought the nicest dress available and even lost fifteen pounds. It doesn't matter though, because that bitch is gonna be tight when you put it on! Not only that, but after five bridesmaids all take turns trying to figure out how to button, zip, or lace you into it, something is bound to give. That's when things get old-school, and the trusty needle and thread make their appearance. It doesn't happen every time, but it happens enough that I keep a sewing kit in my equipment bag just in case.

8. One of the rings ends up on the wrong finger during the ceremony. It's typical for one or both of you to have trouble getting the ring on. Even more common is the flash of panic when standing there trying to determine which hand is the correct one. The situation usually plays out the same. There's a bit of a pause up at the altar, some awkward laughter, and then a big sigh of relief that the ring made it to the target. Sometimes the bride or groom will give up, leaving the ring on the first knuckle. Either way, the big secret is to not worry about it. There might be a hundred people watching, but few notice, and if they do, it's a great story for the cocktail hour.

9. Neither you nor anyone else will remember how to bustle the dress. I picked on the guys earlier, but this one is as close to a wedding proverb as you can get. After the ceremony, it's time to take the back of the wedding gown from fairy-princess length to a more manageable dancing length. All dresses with long trains have this feature, and they all work differently. Those few moments between the end of the family photos and the introduction of the wedding party into the reception can be frantic and frustrating. Especially when a half-dozen concerned and helpful women are packed around the bride's backside like hens at feeding time. Lifting the back of the dress, straight up to the sky, everyone points and searches under there for some blinking neon sign explaining what to do next. Your mind drifts back a few months when the lady at the dress salon showed you and your maid of honor how to do it. She made it seem so simple, so effortless, but neither of you paid attention. You were both having too much fun discussing plans for the upcoming bachelorette weekend. If you've ever seen a group of men crowded around the open hood of a broken down car pointing at the engine, their foreheads wrinkled into an expression that says, "Hmm, I'm not sure what that part does, but give that thing over there a twist and see what happens," then you know exactly what this scene behind the dress looks like.

10. When you are in a public place in your wedding dress, strangers will honk, yell, stare, and take pictures. It's like people think you're famous. They are mostly well-wishers. But some people act like they've never seen a bride before, and they end up taking more pictures than I do. In the South, there's also the proverbial redneck in the muddy truck who drives by and yells, "Don't do it!" Gotta love that guy.

11. Little girls will think you are a fairy princess. Seriously, what happens at the end of every fairy-princess story? She gets married. What does she look like? She looks just like you when you're all dressed up. So don't feel self-conscious about the wide-eyed amazement of those under age twelve, who think that you have magical powers. They are staring at you in hopes of seeing wings sprout and watching you fly away into happily-ever-after land.

12. You are likely to yell at your mother for no good reason. Mother- daughter dynamics are mysterious at best. So many emotions and expectations lay beneath the surface that a boilover is inevitable. At some weddings, it is obvious that it's the MOB's wedding; the bride is just in it for the open bar. Sometimes the MOB is so worried about making everything perfect that she stresses everyone out. The bride attack comes out of nowhere in the form of a terse exclamation of, "It's fine Mom, relax!" and is gone just as quickly. Sometimes though, a snippy remark sets the tone for the day, and everyone scatters for fear of setting off the bride again.

13. One or more of your bridesmaids will thoroughly annoy you all day long.

Every wedding party has one bridesmaid who refuses to believe that every little thing that happens on the wedding day is not about her. At some point during the day, you will find yourself thinking, "Why the hell does she keep trying to stress me out? Can't she just shut up about that one cloud over there and quit complaining about how cold she is? If she doesn't shut up about how these high heels I'm 'making them wear' are wrecking her feet, I will take them off and beat her bitch-ass down with them!" That's also the point when you'll struggle to rationalize your choice of bridesmaids. You'll think, "I doubt I'll even know her in three years. I only asked her to do this so I'd have the same number of bridesmaids as there are groomsmen. If I had this to do over again, bitch would be out!"

Chapter 3
Bless Your Heart

Having lived in the South all of my life, I could write an entire chapter on just these three words. If you have been in the South for more than an hour, you have no doubt heard the expression, "Bless your heart." The majority of the time, you can expect this phrase to be uttered by a sweet little old lady with a smooth Southern drawl. To those unfamiliar with the nuance of Southern culture, this "blessing" might sound like a sincere wish for a person's circumstances to change for the positive. This couldn't be further from the truth.

In the South (at least where I have lived), it is a generally accepted practice that you can say disparaging things about a person you know as long as somewhere within the insult you insert a sincere enough sounding, "bless his (or her) heart." It's perfectly fine to pass harsh judgment on another, so long as you end with an insincere cliché wishing them well.

A wedding is a great opportunity for family and friends from the couple's past and present to gather and pass judgment on every move made by the people hosting the event. Whether intended or not, weddings put the couple and their families on display for everyone to see. Style, social skills, hospitality, tastes, and manners, or lack thereof, are noted by those in attendance, some of whom are less forgiving than others in their assessments. Here are some examples:

- Have you seen Charlene yet? She's a pretty girl, but, bless her heart, that dress makes her look six months pregnant.

- I hope Eugene can find a good manual labor job to support the two of them. Bless his heart, that poor boy has less sense than a bowl of burnt grits.
- Wasn't that just the sweetest first dance you've ever seen? That Luanne has all the grace and poise of a Mack dump truck bless her heart.

Another equally popular usage of the phrase is the stand alone, "bless your heart." This format is used when the speaker can think of nothing nice to say. Sometimes what they want to say is too harsh even for a "bless your heart" to cancel it out. The key is that when saying the words, the speaker needs to do a good job of feigning concern and sympathy. Every Southerner intuitively knows that it is vital for a proper "blessing" to sound sincere and nurturing.

Southern vernacular also allows for a special modifier to be added to the end of the stand alone "bless your heart" that really drives the point home. It's best used for those times when you want to call someone an idiot to their face and have them walk away feeling great about it. In those situations, once the "bless your heart" has been successfully delivered, simply follow up with a heartfelt "I'll be praying for you." How great are you right now? You're blessing them and praying for them. They have no idea you can't stand them and are going to tell everyone they know what a kind and sincere person you are.

It's awfully liberating to know that you can verbalize any deep-seated angst or frustration about someone you know as long as you remember this fundamental phrase. It's the sole reason why Southern Baptists have no need to go to confession the way Catholics do. They can simply say: "bless her heart," bake a casserole, and move on with their day guilt-free. It should be noted however that this is a true and authentic Southern phenomenon and only works if the speaker has a noticeable drawl. Don't go blessing anyone with your Boston accent or you're going to start a fight.

The following stories are ones that, after reflecting on the circumstances and choices that were made, I can't help but shake my head and utter those three little words.

Most Memorable Quotes Ever

"Oh my God, I'm freaking out! I've never done this, what do I do? Oh my God, oh my God, oh my God!"

> Bride yelling frantically to her sister in reference to her soon-to-expire virginity.

Don't Drop the g

The *g* is precious and should never be taken for granted. While it is powerful, it is also delicate and must be protected no matter the effort required. One careless move, and the *g* might slip and shatter. Then all is lost.

You see, the letter *g* is not only the seventh letter of the English alphabet; it's also the seventh letter in the word *wedding*. If it is compromised, I can assure you it will be sorely missed. Guests will not experience a wedding, but rather its inbred half-cousin the *weddin'*. Unlike their more formal counterpart, weddin's are a casual affair. You will think you're watching a reality show in which the Beverly Hillbillies get together with the Real Housewives of East Cackalacky. They all go to a craft fair and then a fish fry. Drama ensues and someone ends up speeding off in a really loud truck.

To the untrained eye a weddin' may be hard to spot. On the surface, it has similar components, like flowers, bridal parties, food, and a cake. It also has customs such as toasts, traditional dances, and bouquet tosses. The difference between the two is all in the execution.

Weddin's are where you find the reception tables covered in faux silk ivy from the craft store. Among these lovely arrangements, one might notice an assortment of small plaster cherubs spray-painted gold to add just the right level of opulence. Champagne flutes are far too high brow for a weddin'. Luckily, this problem can be solved by purchasing a couple of short crystal candlesticks at the dollar store and hot gluing them to the bottom of a mason jar. (I'm so not kidding. Go to the Internet and search for "hillbilly wine glass.")

A weddin' is where the groom's entire family needs a smoke break before they can even think about taking family photos. The eight-year-old flower girl is obsessed with being Honey Boo Boo. I can't make the guys walk too far for pictures because every single groomsman is one sausage and gravy biscuit away from 300 pounds and their first heart attack. At a weddin' you'll find that the cake is falling over even before the reception begins. No one is mad, though, because the bride's mother's Sunday-school teacher made it. She even went the extra mile and rented the little fountain for it. It is also perfectly normal that immediately after the ceremony, the weddin' party and guests all get rid of those stuffy suits and dresses to change into more comfortable shorts, T-shirts, and flip-flops.

When a photographer is just starting out, it's a safe bet that he or she will get at least a few weddin's in the beginning. Those first weddin's are not to be avoided, as they often hold the most memorable stories of a photographer's career. I still fondly recall one of our first weddin's. What stuck out to me was that even though it was the late 1990s, Kevin, the groom clearly owned a time machine that kept him living in the mid 1980s. Still rocking a mullet, he was the spitting image of the jock character from every Brat Pack movie ever made in the decade of decadence.

All day he kept on about how he was ready to "get out of this monkey suit and back in my WrestleMania t-shirt." To save a few bucks, Kevin passed on hiring a DJ and decided instead to make a mix tape of his favorite 80s tunes. To this day, I can still envision the scene of their cake-cutting perfectly. We were in the tiny basement fellowship hall of their country church. The discord of dozens of simultaneous conversations between friends and family members was drowning out the sounds from Kevin's mix tape. At the suggestion of the church director, the couple made their way over to the cake. I was kneeling down in front of the cake table to get an interesting angle and focused on Kevin and his bride. As the guests turned their attention toward the cake at the front of the room, the conversations subsided and allowed the magical sounds of "Tainted Love" by Soft Cell to be the soundtrack of the moment.

> Once I ran to you (I ran)
> Now I'll run from you
> This tainted love you've given
> I give you all a boy could give you
> Take my tears and that's not nearly all
> Oh…tainted love
> Tainted love
>
> Now I know I've got to
> Run away I've got to
> Get away
>
> Don't touch me please
> I cannot stand the way you tease
> I love you though you hurt me so
> Now I'm going to pack my things and go…

I scanned the room to see if I was the only one who found what was happening in front of all of us to be the most ironic thing ever. To this day, I cannot hear that song without being transported right back to that little hall with its magical cake-cutting moment. Bless their hearts!

Pain Meds and Mimosas

I hung up the phone and looked at Meridith in disbelief.

"That was her mom. Apparently Marissa has been in the hospital for the last three days and is signing herself out right now."

It was two hours before Marissa's wedding was to take place, and we had been at the hotel for over a half-hour wondering where everyone was. It was summertime in Charleston, South Carolina, and we were anticipating a grand Southern garden wedding. After the call, we weren't sure what to expect.

Marissa arrived with her parents a half-hour later, and Meridith followed her to the bridal suite to photograph her preparations. The mood in the room was light but quiet. Marissa was moving slowly as she began her makeup routine. When it came time to get her into the dress, Meridith noticed marks on her upper chest visible above the bodice. They were the kind of circular impressions you get from suction-cup sensors that monitor your heart. It's not like she had sprained a wrist, or a bad migraine; whatever put her in the hospital must have been a big deal. As Marissa sat down to have her makeup applied, the hairdresser came up with the genius idea that, instead of putting Marissa's hair up as originally planned, they would use her long brown locks to cover those marks on her chest. As girls in the room talked about what was going on with Marissa, Meridith learned that she had gone to the emergency room a few days before because of pain in her leg that turned out to be a blood clot, which could potentially travel from her leg to her lung. If left untreated, it could mean a quick and certain death. Even though she had been in the hospital for a few days and had surgery the day before, Marissa treated the situation as if it were a minor inconvenience. She was getting married one way or another. I've learned that very little comes between a girl and her wedding plans.

Meridith urgently texted me from the bridal suite to meet her out in the hallway near the lobby. With wide eyes she told me, "This girl has been through some crazy stuff over the past few days. They had to put some kind of filter in her leg to keep the blood clot from killing her. I just saw her take some pain pills, and I'm not sure if she'll be up for pictures."

It looked like there was a slim chance that any photos were going to happen prior to the ceremony. The only reason we were there was to photograph Marissa's wedding, and now we had to figure out how to do that within the circumstances we were given. How would we salvage this? I needed a new plan and questioned Meridith.

"Does she seem like she's feeling better after the meds? Do you think she'll be able to go outside later?"

"I can't really tell." Meridith said. "She seems fine but is moving slow. She doesn't seem too out of it from the pain medicine, and the weird thing is that no one else around her is treating her like she is fragile."

"Well if they're not concerned, should we be?"

"I just don't want to be one of those people you see on the news who had a client die during a photo shoot and have people say we pushed a fragile girl too far."

"Yeah," I said, "the media would have a field day. Can you see the headline of that story? Parted by Death on Her Wedding Day—Photographer Goes too Far."

"That's not funny." Meridith snapped.

"It's only not funny if it actually happens."

I do take this kind of thing seriously. One of the most troubled memories I carry from my life in commercial photography was the day that Tony, our fashion stylist, suddenly began acting sluggish and clumsy during a lingerie shoot. Tony had a lively personality and always moved at twice the speed of everyone else. We were about three hours into our shoot and were setting up for the final shot. One second Tony was adjusting the model's bra, the next I noticed him stumble and freeze right where he stood, looking around with a dazed expression. An hour later as everyone was packing to leave, the whole crew was concerned and encouraging Tony to go straight to a doctor. He brushed us off and said he was fine.

"If I feel bad tomorrow I'll go to the doctor and get checked out," he slurred.

Tony fell into a coma that night. It turned out that he was having a stroke right there on set; all of us saw it happen and had no idea. Tony's story did not end well.

With hindsight being twenty-twenty, I am sensitive to situations where someone's health could be on the line while they stubbornly forge ahead telling me that they are fine.

The one thing I couldn't understand with Marissa's situation was that neither Eric, the groom, or any of her family seemed outwardly nervous or worried about her current condition. It turned out this had been happening for years with Marissa. A hospital stay, a small surgical procedure, and life went on. I guess if you go through that enough, it becomes routine.

But Meridith and I were freaking out. Finding out that our client was in such a precarious state of health forced us to reevaluate our photo plans. There was no way we were going to do our usual schedule and take this bride all over the hotel grounds for great scenery. So how do we create memorable photos while keeping Marissa comfortable and safe?

Meridith and I were a mess the whole day, afraid that something we asked of her would exhaust her and she would pass out. We walked on eggshells and covered all of the normal types of photos. We kept reading Marissa and her family for any signs that we were pushing too hard. On top of our complete anxiety, we still felt the pressure to deliver the level of images they expected from us. For all we knew, these could be the last pictures of her, and that's an added level of stress. We've been in those situations before, and it's not easy to be creative with such a heavy feeling of finality looming over.

Marissa needed several breaks between photos to rest, but I was beginning to feel like the day would be a success. Except for the smiles. Bless her heart, the girl had just been through surgery the day before and was on some strong pain medication. Every time I asked her to look at the camera, the best she could do was to look right through me with a distant expression, completely void of emotion. You know the kind of smile that kids do when adults prompt them to "Say cheese"? The one where their mouth is saying, "cheese", but their eyes are practically yawning. Needless to say, the eyes did not match what the mouth was doing.

I knew that the resulting images would look emotionally disconnected at best. I pulled out every trick in my bag to get her expressions looking more natural: asking Eric to make her laugh, having them look away from the camera, even asking her not to smile in a few. No matter the direction given, it was all the same expression. Distant, vacant eyes with a big toothy grin. I had little choice but to roll with it.

It's true that some folks just have awkward smiles, but that wasn't normally the case with Marissa. I photographed her and Eric's engagement session just a few months before. At that time, her natural expressions and effortless smile made her eyes sparkle with enthusiasm. It was all very believable. So I knew that it was the pain meds and fatigue that put us in our current situation.

The ceremony gave us a few moments to take stock of how things were going. The service went smoothly, though Marissa was still weak and had to sit for all of it, which meant that Eric was also seated. As they sat facing each other and holding hands, I wondered if the guests knew about her condition or if they were thinking that sitting at the altar was some new wedding fad. We wondered if anyone outside of the family knew about her recent hospital stay and if anyone else shared our anxiety. I knew she must be exhausted after the last few hours of being "on" for the cameras and her guests. We even thought that she might need a break or a nap between the ceremony and reception, but she was determined to enjoy herself, and we were sending every bit of positive energy available in her direction to help will her through the day incident free.

Immediately after the ceremony, the halls of the hotel filled with celebratory buzz and excitement. Since this was a morning wedding, the hotel staff began passing champagne and mimosas around to the guests on silver trays. Guests crowded around the newlyweds. The hallway overflowed with bright morning sunlight and the energy of hundreds of lively conversations all happening at once. Meridith and I were going about our work of capturing candid moments and breathing a huge sigh of relief that everyone made it through this thing alive so far. When we saw Marissa take a mimosa from the tray in the midst of the revelry, we figured she would pass it to her groom Eric, or do a cute toast for the camera. Instead, she put it to her lips, turned the bottom up, and it was gone in three gulps. Time stopped for me for a brief moment as I watched Marissa's maid of honor hand her two more pain pills, which she washed down with a second mimosa. I knew then that we were in for an interesting evening.

A half-dozen family groups and two more mimosas later, we wrapped up the formal photos and it was reception time. The party was like any other reception. Eric and his bride danced and had a great time. If Marissa was in pain, no one knew it, including her. While she was dancing the night away, she was drinking the night away too.

I was really worried for this girl, but I seemed to be the only one. So far I have a spotless record of not having any clients carried from the reception in an ambulance, and was hoping to keep it that way. But what can you do? Do I just walk up and say, "Hey, I noticed that you seem to be taking a lot of pain medication and mixing it with alcohol. That seems like it has the potential to not end well for you." No one in her family including her new husband seemed concerned, but I also realized that no one else was paying attention to her as much as we were.

There are so many distractions and great people to talk with at a wedding that while Eric saw her take a pill three hours before and her mom saw her take two a few hours before that, we were the only ones who witnessed all of them, plus the ones she snuck out of her maid of honor's purse throughout the day. The girl was determined to enjoy her day and no silly brush with death was going to impede that.

Eric and Marissa seemed to have a great time and surprised us by staying until the very end of the reception. I was so relieved when they drove away at the end of the night and everything seemed fine. Meridith and I had been so tied up in knots all day long thinking that we would have to call 911. To have nothing bad happen was a huge relief. We were both exhausted from being on pins and needles and were ecstatic that the day was over.

A month went by before I heard from Marissa's mom. It turned out that about two hours after she waved goodbye to her guests and left the reception, Eric had to call an ambulance and rush her to the emergency room. She spent the next week in intensive care and remained in the hospital another three weeks recovering from all the damage inflicted on her body while she was numb from the meds and alcohol on her wedding day.

Most Memorable Quotes Ever

"Go on! You'd better roll your ass out there!"

> The Father of the bride yelling to a female guest in a wheelchair as the single ladies lined up to catch the bouquet.

I'll Be Right Back

I've never seen anyone left at the altar. We've had plenty of weddings called off the week or two before, but never the day of. There have been close calls when we saw either the bride or groom freaking out more than normal just before the ceremony. I'm talking a level of freaking out where everyone was asked to leave the room and the groom and his father have an intense man-to-man discussion. When you see the minister called into one of those, you get the feeling you might be going home early. But just like in the movies, things turn around and only those who were there to see it happen ever knew about it.

Rose and Michael were having what we refer to as the "standard format." In the South that means a 20-minute Protestant ceremony at a beautiful church followed by a traditional country club reception with all the formalities. When we arrived at Rose's hotel a few hours before the ceremony to start photography, she was in the makeup chair. The bridesmaids were getting into their dresses and trying to get their hair done like the hot actress of the moment in the latest issue of *People Magazine*.

Rose was visibly distressed. She kept asking to "take a minute," saying that she just didn't feel well. She would go into another room to lie down on a sofa. Five or ten minutes would pass, and she would rejoin the group smiling as if nothing was wrong. This went on for an hour, and I wondered if she was nervous or really sick.

We had just photographed her engagement session a few weeks before and she was very comfortable in front of the camera. Some people become complete basket cases or self-conscious because all eyes will be on them. This girl wasn't that type, so I didn't feel like I was the one bringing on her condition. I thought maybe she *was* sick. We'll slow down the pace, get her to the ceremony, and hope for the best.

In a standard format wedding, there's rarely any drama, and Rose and Michael's ceremony was as standard as they come. Everyone was seated. Six bridesmaids walked down the aisle followed by a cute ring bearer, then an even cuter flower girl. The doors to the sanctuary closed, and Rose's father stepped up to take her arm. They exchanged brief smiles, and he said something funny to diffuse the weight of the moment. The lead church lady cracked the door open to give the thumbs up to the organist, and the music began at a deafening volume as the doors hurled open. All eyes were on Rose and her father. The two church ladies took turns fluffing the train and straightening the veil more than seemed necessary. As the processional began, I can only guess what was going through Rose's and her father's minds at this point. They both walked slowly, staring into the happy and smiling faces of people they may or may not know.

It seems like it would be an out-of-body type of experience. You have to think about it this way: The first few aisles they pass will most likely be empty except for the people who show up late and sneak in the side door while the bridesmaids are walking down the aisle. Once Rose and her father pass the late crowd, they reach the middle section of pews, which is a mixture of work people, grad-school people from a few years ago, and friends of the couple's parents whom neither the bride nor the groom have likely met before. It's a full two-thirds of the way down the aisle before father and daughter lock eyes with faces they both recognize, because close family usually sits at the front. In talking with past clients though, few actually remember that walk. I guess that's a good thing since a large part of the reason I am there is to help prove that it did happen.

As Rose arrived at the altar and stood beside Michael, I was rooting for her. In making it down the aisle, she had just completed the most emotionally intense moment of the day. Often the anticipation of that instant when the doors open is the hardest part. Once that walk is over, it's easy from there. I was certain that in terms of nervous jitters, the worst was over. Again, we followed the standard format where the Minister said words while Rose and Michael held hands and then repeated the words. Just before the minister held up the rings, Rose put her hand to her mouth, and her shoulders slumped forward. I was stuck in the balcony about as far as you could be from where they were standing, but I could tell she was panicked. Her head darted left and right around the room looking for relief or for an exit. In what sounded like a heaving grunt I heard her say, "Hold on!" She covered her mouth and bolted through the side door as fast as she could.

Everyone was stunned because, aside from the bridesmaids, no one else had experienced the episodes earlier in the day. Not knowing if Rose's hasty exit was due to physical or emotional causes, the minister put his hand on Michael's shoulder and told him to stay right there; he would go attend to her. The minister and maid of honor, Stephanie, walked briskly out the door of the sanctuary and into the adjacent hallway. The other 160 of us sat there staring at Michael as he stared back and rocked nervously from heel to toe.

When the minister and Stephanie found Rose, she was on the floor, crying, dry heaving, and struggling to get the words out that she thought she was going to start vomiting. As the minister tried to sooth Rose by having her take deep breaths, Stephanie went to get her some water. The minister asked Rose if she was in pain. She replied that she wasn't but had been sick with nausea all day. That's when Stephanie, returning with water, leaned in close to Rose and whispered, "Are you absolutely sure you're not pregnant?"

I only knew that this exchange took place because even though all of us were sitting and staring straight ahead in the most awkward silence imaginable, we could hear everything over the minister's lapel microphone. It was still on and even though we couldn't see them, the sound was coming through loud and clear over the speakers, with every whisper booming loudly throughout the sanctuary.

Michael's eyebrows shot straight up into outer space. Ten minutes into his own wedding and there he was, left standing alone at the altar, staring at his parents on one side of the aisle, Rose's family on the other. And now he's hearing over a loudspeaker that he might be a daddy. It was less than a nanosecond before one of the other bridesmaids ran off the stage and nearly broke down the door to get to the minister and that microphone. After that, there was no more sound, just silence and a groom standing all by himself up at the altar, staring at a room full of people who were completely paralyzed with mortification. Five very long silent minutes passed before Rose returned to the altar with the minister and her bridesmaids, recomposed and ready to forge ahead as if nothing had happened.

She took Michael's hand, and they picked up where they left off exchanging rings. Everything returned to normal. The standard format was back in effect.

I leaned over to Meridith, who was with me in the balcony, and whispered, "The first trimester's a bitch!"

She lost her composure and started laughing, but it was okay because by then the organ was playing a solo during the lighting of the unity candle, and no one heard a thing out of us.

Rose got through the rest of the ceremony like a champ. She did have to take a few more breaks between the post-ceremony photos and the reception. That made me realize that it had nothing to do with nerves, which then made me think that she probably was pregnant and planned on telling everyone that it happened on the honeymoon. I hear that one a lot.

The weird part was, Meridith and I would have bet good money on her being pregnant. It happens a lot more than you think, but at least five years went by before they had their first child. Maybe something from the rehearsal dinner didn't agree with her, or maybe that dress was just too tight. Either way, we will never forget Rose.

Bad Moon Rising

When you're new at something, you don't know what's normal until you've been around the block a few times. That's part of the reason I wrote this book. I've been doing this long enough that I see emotional people, drunk people, irrational, rowdy, and out-of-control people nearly every weekend. I forget that not everyone acts that way. When I share stories with others outside of my profession, they are shocked to hear about some of the things that I have witnessed over the years.

I wasn't always jaded. For the first few years as wedding photographers, Meridith and I were admittedly naive. We assumed that the format for our work would be basic and predictable. The couple would show up looking fabulous, get married, have some cake, and dance a little. We would be there to take pictures so that years later they could prove to their grandkids that they were indeed once young and hip. We simply didn't anticipate all of the variables that come into play at weddings.

Early in our career, we learned that nothing is predictable, and we should be ready for anything. We received an intense tutorial in expectation management at what was probably our fifth wedding.

Both the bride and groom were from Los Angeles, but because the bride's grandfather lived in Greensboro and he was in poor health, she decided to have her wedding there and fly in all of the guests. That's about all we knew going into the shoot. Since they didn't live anywhere near us, we had never met them and had no idea what to expect.

We arrived at the Grandover Resort and entered the suite just as the bride, Michelle, was passing out large gift bags to each of her eight bridesmaids. I was impressed. Each girl received a personalized Prada handbag. Not the Canal Street knock-off Prada, but the actual oh-my-God-is-that-really-the-price Prada.

Meridith shot an envious glance across the room at me with eyes that said, "You don't buy me Prada bags."

Tucked inside each handbag was a handwritten note from Michelle, accompanied by a personalized charm necklace in a little blue box from that place in New York that's named after a girl. Actually it's named after a guy, but he had a girly last name. Anyway, it didn't take long before we got the impression that money wasn't a concern for this couple or any of their friends. You learn a lot when you are amongst the girl talk and hear where they go, what they do, the things they like, and how they spend their time. By the conversations going on it became obvious that these peeps were living large and loving life in L.A. I guessed that Michelle was probably in her mid-twenties and seemed young to be loaded with money she made herself. Having not met Brian, the groom, I wondered if Michelle was marrying herself a sugar daddy.

I went downstairs to meet up with Brian and his guys to begin photographing them. It wasn't hard to spot nine guys in tuxedos talking loudly at the bar. Even before getting to where the group was seated, I learned that Brian was house shopping because he just bought a new Maserati, which meant that he had outgrown his four-car garage. I remember feeling completely cheated in that moment because Meridith was upstairs and I didn't get the chance to look at her and say, "You never bought me a Maserati."

I quickly realized that Brian and his groomsmen were a rowdy, fun-loving bunch of dudes. Surprisingly, these guys were young too. Not the cigar-smoking, gray-haired fifty year olds I anticipated. It was obvious from their stories that nobody's mommy or daddy was paying for this wedding. That led me to my second incorrect assumption of the day. It was the late 1990s and I assumed that since they were from California, they must have been a part of some incredible startup company and had the good fortune to cash out before the dot-com bubble went bust.

When I finally got them to agree to go outside for photos, they had already been at the bar for an hour and were good and buzzed. There were nine of them, each one with the attention span of a spastic squirrel. When we began creating images, I tried my best not to lose their focus. Several of them would begin conversations in the middle of a shot. It was all I could do to get a few to pause long enough to look at the camera. I kept them moving from one scene to the next so that no one would wander off if they saw something shiny.

Back in the bride's suite, Michelle put on her dress, which is when Meridith realized that she had the largest breasts we have ever seen on a non-cartoon person. Meridith had no idea before then because when we arrived Michelle had on a big, slouchy sweatshirt. You have to understand that I'm not one to fixate on women's body parts or even talk about breasts. But with the plunging bodice style of dress she chose, it was like cleavage-fest 1998. It wasn't just that her chest was large. It's normal for big girls to have breasts sized proportionate to the rest of their body. Michelle, however, was not a big girl, and it was obvious that her breasts were made to be that large. There is no natural way to end up looking like she did. You have to see a doctor about that sort of thing. Even Meridith couldn't help but gawk in astonishment. I swear those things had their own atmosphere with satellites orbiting. Seriously.

Other stuff made Meridith just as curious as I was. All day long Michelle rested her hands on the tops of her breasts, as if she needed to hold them down. She might take them away for a moment to pick something up, but soon after, her hands would unconsciously return to her breasts, much the same as a pair of parentheses might wrap themselves around humorous subtext. It looked like she was doing the sign language version of: check it, these are my boobs. It was weird to us that her hands were always there, and it was a totally unconscious thing on her part. The other thing that Meridith was struggling with was that Michelle always had either a cigarette in one hand or a drink in the other. Finding the pretty shot in a situation like that was proving to be difficult. Michelle was also smoking and cursing like a sailor while in her dress. We're not offended by bad language, but it was kind of a visual disparity to see an attractive person in a beautiful dress talking and acting that way. It's like the discrepancy you'd experience if you met a four-year-old girl with a Darth Vader voice.

Meridith was raised to be a prim and proper Southern belle, and this whole experience was out of her comfort zone. She kept reminding herself that Michelle wasn't a Southern girl. She was from L.A. and only chose this place because her family lived here. Meridith made peace with it by telling herself, "This is certainly not what we're used to, but let's just do our job and be prepared to look away when the top of that poor dress gives up from all the pressure. We don't have to be best friends with people to make them look good in pictures."

While Meridith was finishing with the ladies in the bridal suite, I was still outside wrapping up photos with the guys. The last half-hour had proven to be rough. The guys were not allowing my little photo shoot to interrupt their party–in-progress. So I thanked them for letting me take their photos and told them that they were free to return to the bar.

One of the groomsmen looked at me indignantly and said, "Hey, we didn't get the one with us mooning the camera."

I said, "Really?"

"Oh yeah, we've got to do that. We always do that. Come on guys, let's go."

I was trying to convince myself that he was probably kidding and any second the other guys would just take him back to the bar. My hopes were dashed when he turned to the group, raised his hands in the air, and said "Let's do this for Michelle!"

As the guys lined up for the shot, Meridith was walking over to let me know that Michelle and the bridesmaids were dressed and ready for me to take their photos.

"What are they doing?" she asked.

"They want to moon the camera," I said as I rolled my eyes.

"Seriously?"

I figured that they would line up and the one guy who had the idea would go all out while the others just humored him but wouldn't really give a full-on moon. Besides, Brian's dad was there, and surely he would rein this in. Unfortunately for me, they were all into it and ready to make some memories.

So they did. Just a few hundred feet from the towering resort with its restaurant veranda full of diners, right there on the eighteenth green, nine guys in tuxes dropped their pants to the ground, flipped their jackets up over their backs, bent over and grabbed their ankles shining their bright hairy asses right at my camera.

Now, there is a tasteful way to do just about anything. Even a group of guys mooning the camera could be done with a subatomic spec of class. Perhaps a little shine of the cheeks and a brief flash-o-crack from under the coattails. But that wasn't what was happening. For some reason these guys decided that they needed full on sun shining where the sun is not supposed to shine, and they were way too proud of it. Standing there for what seemed like far too long with nine butt cracks staring back at us, blazing bright in the afternoon sun, Meridith threw her hand up, let out a proper Southern "Oh Lord!" and took off in the other direction.

This was back in the day when I was shooting film with a big medium-format professional camera. There was no auto focus. There was no auto anything, so I had to manually focus on those butts. Unlike today, there was no option for retouching any of the hairy, dangly nastiness that was going through my camera lens at that moment. One dude was even doing a cheek spread. I thought about just clicking the shutter so it made the sound and they would think I took the picture.

Then I thought, "What are the people at the lab going to think? Can I get in trouble for this?" I made a split-second decision: this situation can't be recreated later, thank goodness, so give the people what they want. I made two exposures, told them we were finished for now, and walked back to the resort to reevaluate my career options. The thought of photographing screaming babies and cat calendars suddenly had more appeal than in years past.

Toward the end of the day more pieces of this puzzle fell into place when we learned that Brian owned an adult-entertainment multimedia company and Michelle, along with all of the wedding party, worked for the company as, well, "video performers." You're getting the idea, right? After finding this out, Meridith and I were biting our nails anticipating what might happen next. Would there be any other performances that evening? What would happen when the alcohol began to flow at the party? Were we about to become porn-star photographers?

Lucky for us, everyone behaved better than expected for the remainder of the event. Even after the wedding I was unsure whether I should show the couple the two mooning photos. But I did. They loved them and even requested that one be included in the album! I just think how different things would be if I shot that wedding now. I would probably be much more entertained than I was back then. The mooning part would still be weird, but I would figure out other ways to harness the group's energy and enthusiasm and use them in a more productive way.

Most Memorable Quotes Ever

"When I first sat down to write this toast, I wasn't sure I was a good person to be giving out marriage advice. But I stand here tonight with my wife and two ex-wives in the same room, and no fights have broken out. So I'm feeling pretty good."

William R.—father of the bride

No More Pictures!

From the email address alone it was obvious that she would be an interesting client. Having not met her in person, receiving an inquiry from: freakynasty@----.com conjured up all sorts of colorful characters in my imagination and had me more than a little curious.

It was late fall when they booked me. Even though their wedding was not until May, we decided to go ahead and get together to shoot Katy and John's engagement session. We met at a park near where they lived in Charlotte and had a good time getting to know each other. This was the first time I had met them in person and was expecting at least a little freaky with perhaps a hint of nasty. Katy wore a green sweater with jeans tucked into light-brown leather boots. John wore jeans and a dark blue button down with the sleeves rolled up. Not the least bit freaky. I left the session with good photos, but I was disappointed. They both seemed totally normal. No freakiness, no nastiness, no crazy story to share with Meridith when I returned; just normal, regular people-ness, which made me even more curious about that email address.

I figured that maybe the address was leftover from a college sorority dare or some other frivolous peer-pressure thing. Katy's wedding day arrived, and we began the same as always. We met her and the ladies in their hotel room and began photographing Katy having her makeup and hair done. It was hard to ignore the amount of booze that was flowing freely. It's normal for the party to begin early with some champagne, but this was a whole different vibe. There were bottles of Jack Daniel's, vodka, and lots of beer around, all being consumed heavily.

Taking the edge off your nerves with a glass or two of wine or champagne is one thing. We see that all the time, and it can be helpful to get people's minds off their anxiety. But for anyone in the wedding party to get completely lushed out before the ceremony has never gone down well in our past observations. After an hour and a half of shooting just the hair and makeup, we could see where the situation was headed. We began to feel some nervousness about what the rest of the day would be like. Would we be able to get the shots we needed with the bride if she was in less-than-sober condition? Would she make it through the ceremony? We had at least another eight hours of scheduled activities for that day. At this rate, I just couldn't imagine her being able to maintain sobriety for that long.

At the church, we readied our cameras for Katy's arrival and hoped that there wouldn't be any delays. Based on what we had seen from this group already, it would not have surprised us if they made a quick stop into the liquor store to restock their supply before the wedding. The limo pulled up to the church. The driver opened the door and Katy emerged with her dad. For the first time that day, I saw her without a drink in her hand. She seemed lucid and alert, and we proceeded with photos as usual. I was impressed. Katy was maybe a hundred ten pounds and, for as much as she had been drinking, she held the alcohol well. We completed photos of the ladies without incident, and they went into the room where they would hide out until the ceremony. The beer and vodka came out again and was enjoyed by all.

Everyone assembled for the ceremony and the proceedings went just like they should. The guests sat down, the music got loud, the doors opened, and the bride walked in. Everything seemed very normal. Then as Katy stood there at the altar with her hands in John's, she began to sway. After having been in constant motion for most of the day, she was now in front of a few hundred people and standing absolutely still. Or so she thought. We had cameras in two different positions. From the back of the church you could see the whole scene, including the couple, the wedding party, and guests. As usual, the couple stood with their backs to the guests, which is why we were also in the choir loft. From the choir loft we could see their faces.

Katy's expression was one of very distant thought. She did a good job of playing sober, but you could tell that her mind was elsewhere. I can only imagine the concentration it took to keep repeating, "Just keep standing, just keep standing!"

Then she started swaying. Every time they would go into a prayer, she would close her eyes and begin an epic struggle with gravity. Once the prayer was over, she would correct herself a bit and sway only slightly less. She spent the entire ceremony looking like she was blowing in a breeze.

We have worked weddings where groomsmen or bridesmaids have passed out, falling out onto the floor and making a big scene. We were certain this would be our first bride to do so. The way she looked and swayed all pointed to one result: she was going down! Fortunately, we were wrong. Through a combination of Katy's ability to hold it together and a super brief ceremony, she made it out with no major blunders. She was even able to enunciate her vows without slurring too badly. I was impressed. She was truly a professional drunk of the highest order and deserved the admiration of alcoholics everywhere.

After family photos, we headed across town for cocktail hour, and it was game on. It had been almost an hour and a half since these ladies had anything to drink, and they were looking to make up for lost time. At this point Katy was two fisting it with a cocktail in one hand and a beer in the other. At the reception, the introductions and traditional dances concluded and the party officially began. Although I still had not seen where the freaky or the nasty fit in with her, one thing you could say was that the girl liked to party! She was all over the dance floor and having a great time.

At some point in the evening, her parents were either embarrassed or tired of her behavior, and her dad tried to cut off the drinks. As she was at the bar lining up another round of shots, he tried to reason with her and get her a water instead of tequila. She got mad and grabbed three of the shots, ran across the room, and downed all of them before he could get to her. It was getting late and the party was winding down at that point. Everyone was staying at the hotel where the reception was held, so there was no grand exit. Katy's father, visibly disgusted, told us, "There's nothing more to see here. You guys can go ahead and leave."

We were staying at the same hotel as everyone else, so we went up to our room to put our cameras away before going out to the car to get our bags. Once in the elevator, we looked at each other with an expression that said, "What the hell just happened?" We were beat. Not only was it a long day, but it is stressful to spend the day worried about the client compromising the quality of images we'll be able to deliver.

After getting our bags from the car, I returned to the lobby and pushed the elevator button to get back up to our room. When the elevator doors slid open there inside were Katy's mom, her dad, and John, the groom. Mom looked down at the floor, clearly embarrassed. Dad stared straight ahead, his arms crossed and lips tight with an expression of defeat. John just looked straight down at his shoes. In front of them slouched over in a wheelchair was Katy with her head slumped, her eyes closed, and the glistening remnants of her lunch and dinner flowing down the front of her wedding gown toward a bucket sitting in her lap. As the doors opened so did one of her eyes. Upon seeing us she faintly raised a hand and mumbled, "No more pictures."

We both tried our best not to react, avoiding eye contact while giving a slight nod as if to say to her parents, "We're going to pretend this never happened." We stepped back, allowing the doors to close, sending these four sad souls on their way. It was at that point that it all came together for me. It was without a doubt one of the most memorable things I would try hard to forget. I wouldn't say that I was scarred for life, but it certainly was freaky—and it sure was nasty.

It is Kinda Hot in Here

Group dynamics at weddings have always fascinated me. It's fun to show up on the wedding day and see the varied characters our client includes in her group of bridesmaids. Often it's a mix of good friends and family members with the token youngster thrown in as a junior bridesmaid to keep peace with a sibling or parent. The bridesmaid dynamic is tricky because half the time, these different people coming together click well and everything works.

Other times it's obvious that the bride leads a double life because the friend bridesmaids look, speak, and act nothing like the family bridesmaids. It nearly always means dysfunction in the group, not that women in these situations would ever be judgmental (yeah, right). Sometimes it's the prim and proper church family mixed with the bride's wild friends from college who sneak wine into the church and have the others all in a tizzy. Or it could be the bride comes from a tiny country town in the middle of nowhere, and she went out into the world to get a fancy education and fancy friends to go with it. Every wedding provides a little different scenario, but in the most extreme cases it can be an explosive combination, like a wedding we did many years ago.

If you tied me up and interrogated me, I could not recall the bride's name, but I vividly remember a bridesmaid named Elizabeth. This is the reason I remember her: Everyone has hang-ups. Some people refuse to step on cracks in the sidewalk some are obsessed with figuring out how everything in life relates back to the number seven. I tend to pick up on things that don't seem to go together. The grown-up word for what I am sensitive to is *incongruence*. But you're not reading this to learn about grown-up words, are you?

I'll just say that the image that comes to my mind when I hear the name Elizabeth was not reconciling with the bridesmaid in front of me. Every Elizabeth I've ever known until that point had been a quiet girl with a pleasant personality. They have also been attractive, elegant, and modest. You can feel comfortable taking a girl named Elizabeth home to meet the parents. Not this one, though.

The bridesmaids were getting ready in a preschool room down the hall from the church sanctuary. From what I could tell, most of them seemed to be lifelong friends who had known the bride since childhood. Amid the usual chatter reminiscing about the good times they shared with the bride back in college, Elizabeth walked in.

Her first question to the bride was, "Who's that guy Brent from the rehearsal dinner last night? He's not married is he?"

"He's not married, but I'm pretty sure he brought a date," said the bride.

Elizabeth responded, "Mmm hmm, all I know is, date or not, I'm hittin' that shit tonight."

Seeing Elizabeth, then hearing what came out of her mouth was an experience much like when the carpets don't match the drapes (which I suspected was also true). But in this case, the name didn't match the girl. She was clearly a Brandi or a Destiny, maybe even a Kandy, but definitely not an Elizabeth. I was baffled that no one else was seeing this. She was the kind of girl that a guy who has just been tossed out of a long-term relationship wants to meet in a bar on a lonely Thursday night. The kind of girl who would ask him all about his life, and before he knows it, he's waking up to the sun coming thought the blinds of his bedroom smelling like beer and cigarettes. He wonders if it was all a dream until he sees the note propped up on his alarm clock that says, "Last night was fun. You might want to go get tested for stuff."

There was subtle, yet noticeable tension whenever Elizabeth was among the other bridesmaids. She was taller, thinner, and generally prettier than all of them. She didn't flaunt it; she didn't have to. The others in the group recognized it and kept their jealous hatred tucked neatly inside their freshly monogrammed Vera Bradley handbags they were given as their bridesmaids' gifts. The girls were nice to her but kept their distance. To everyone except for the bride, Elizabeth was an outsider. She didn't care, though. She was there to have fun and looking forward to a party.

All was well and good at the wedding until the reception. Elizabeth (a.k.a. Brandi, a.k.a. Destiny, as I began to call her) decided she was going to take a break from her reality and made good friends with the bartender. She was pretty loaded by the time the dance floor opened up, and when it did she was stumbling all over it. She didn't bring a date, so she decided to latch onto every guy close enough to grab. The guys were thinking, "Wow, this is awesome!" until they got that look from their wife or girlfriend that let them know fun time with skank-a-licious was over. Whenever a guy left her, she never missed a beat and would just dance by herself in the middle of the floor. She'd drop it like it was hot until the next unsuspecting guy got close enough to grab.

An hour into the dancing, I heard people talking about her. By this time, Elizabeth's shoes were long gone and she had worked up a sweat shaking that rump with everything she had. Most of the men had gotten wise to what was going on and surrounded the perimeter of the dance floor stacked three-deep to watch the show. I saw one lady yelling at her husband after she saw Elizabeth grinding on him. The older folks were upset because she was dancing inappropriately and making a scene. The guys with dates were nervous because they knew that if she grabbed onto one of them, then the rest of his day was ruined. The photos we were getting on the dance floor were funny but not very dynamic. Just Elizabeth in the middle, dancing in her own little world, completely oblivious. Couples kept a wide distance and decided to shake it down on the outer edge of the dance floor.

The DJ switched up the music and played a song that had just come out a few weeks before, "Hot in Herre," by Nelly. It was only the second time I had heard it played at a reception. The crowd that evening was white—really white. They had no idea what to do with this song. Most of the dance floor cleared out except for maybe six people. As the song was playing, I kept seeing Elizabeth grab her floor length dress, hike it up to the middle of her thigh, and throw herself around. At this stage of drunken delirium, her eyes were closed and she was just flailing around unconsciously to the beat. She was so drunk she didn't realize other people were around at the edge of the dance floor, scowling while avoiding her as if she were green and glowing. As a few in the crowd were singing along with the chorus—"It's getting hot in here, so take off all your clothes"—Elizabeth reached down to her ankles, grabbed the bottom of her dress, and lifted her arms straight up over her head, taking the whole dress up toward the ceiling.

All you could see were legs, panties, hips swinging, and the inside lining of the dress up over her head. Aside from her thong, she was completely bare from her rib cage down. Nowadays I would be shooting the hell out of that, but back then I was a more timid photographer, so I put my camera down in a dramatic fashion to let everyone know I wasn't going to be making memories out of any of this.

I was, however, pleased to verify something that just a few hours before I could only speculate about. Elizabeth did indeed have the obligatory tramp stamp—a butterfly with scrollwork on either side. The crowd froze. The DJ cut the music and dance lights right in the middle of the song so the whole place went dark. Those who were into the dancing and had not yet noticed what was going on behind them walked off the dance floor in disgust.

A few seconds after the music stopped, Elizabeth's dress came down and she looked around with the expression that said, "What just happened?" She stumbled off the dance floor pulling her long sweaty locks out of her face as if she had just woken up from a deep sleep.

We didn't see Elizabeth anymore after that. I assumed the bride or someone got a hold of her and put her in time-out for the rest of the party. Since that was only the second time I had heard that song played at a reception, it created an expectation that another impromptu peep show might someday happen again. It hasn't. But DJs still play it, and I'm still waiting.

Chapter 4
Uninvited Guests

Weddings can bring out the crazy in just about anyone. Jealous ex-boyfriends could show up. Estranged parents or stepparents may decide to show up unannounced just because they can. Then there are those relatives who for whatever reason seem to hate each other. Family and friend dynamics are usually taken into account when the guest list is being finalized and people are invited accordingly. Some will be left off of the guest list because the couple hasn't been in touch with them in years, others because the person will stir up trouble or constantly hit on the bridesmaids. Whatever the reason, there are some people who would take away from the day simply by being there.

There are circumstances when people show up that you never would have anticipated. Sometimes it makes the day more interesting to have a random jogger photo bomb the family group photos. At other times, unexpected visitors can make for a completely awkward situation. Since we are documenting the entire wedding, we don't welcome distractions that make our subjects project unhappy expressions. Our couples don't usually want photos of things or people that didn't relate to the wedding.

Sometimes though, we have no idea who is crashing the party. We might take pictures of them, and funny (or not so funny) stories are shared after our clients view their images. The stories in this chapter focus on unexpected characters who worked themselves into a wedding day.

The Circle of Life

Puerto Vallarta, Mexico, was not at all how I imagined it. I was thinking bright sandy beaches, tropical breezes, and clear blue water. Turns out I was imagining the Bahamas. (I've never been there either; I'm just bad at geography.) The only sandy beach in that town was the ten-by-fifty-foot-strip that our hotel installed for the tourists. Everything else was rocky coastline, which was still beautiful in its own way. The one thing I did get right was that July proved to be as hot and humid as anticipated and, for some reason, Meridith and I had the bright idea to pack dark suits for the wedding. It was also the start of the rainy season, so there were guaranteed afternoon showers nearly every day.

We didn't care about the heat, the rain, or the heavy packs of equipment we were carrying around because the place was visual crack! Whenever I'm fully engaged behind the camera, I get into a zone where all of my other senses shut down in deference to my vision. I experience the whole world through what I see in that viewfinder. My hearing tunes out, I don't notice temperature, and there is no recollection of tastes, smells, or aching muscles. When I'm in the zone, my only reality happens through that camera.

On the day before the wedding, Meridith and I arrived at the villa where our clients, Jessica and Tim, and their families were staying. It was a fascinating complex of free-form rooms and pathways, and I was in awe of the place. Everywhere I looked was vibrant and full of creative details. It was obvious that artists rather than engineers designed the place. The vivid colors, tropical plants, and the Pacific Ocean do wonders for stimulating creativity. This location was one of my all-time favorite places to create photographs.

At eight thirty on the morning of wedding, Meridith and I took a cab from our hotel and returned to the villa to photograph Jessica and Tim as they were getting ready for the first of two ceremonies. They told me that most places in Mexico do not recognize the traditional church ceremonies we are accustomed to in the United States. They like civil ceremonies conducted by a court official, which involves romantic gestures like the bride and groom adding their thumbprints to the marriage license. I guess that's followed by the traditional wiping-off-the-ink ceremony. As enchanting as all of that might sound, Jessica and Tim were both Catholic, and even though they understood that it would not be "official," they wanted a traditional Catholic Mass to be a part of their wedding experience.

By eleven o'clock, everyone in the party was ready to leave the villa and head downtown to the Cathedral of Our Lady of Guadeloupe. Jessica and Tim decided that they would not see each other prior to the ceremony. Tim and his groomsmen arrived separately and were able to duck into a back room of the cathedral. Jessica and the rest of the families followed soon after. Everyone was right on time, but we were all asked to wait outside in the courtyard because a baby was being baptized. We had no problem waiting a few more minutes and creating beautiful images of Jessica outside the church. Everywhere we turned there was gorgeous scenery with weathered stone arches and tropical trees. Eventually the proud family exited with their newly baptized child, and we were allowed inside.

The interior of the cathedral was beautiful. Exactly what I expected: a vast collection of paintings and statues, lots of candles, and gold paint everywhere you looked. For a small downtown area, the place was bustling with activity. While the decoration and architecture were very formal, the energy of the space was decidedly casual. Maybe it was the fact that the couple brought everyone there to have a great time, or maybe it was the tourists walking around in their cargo shorts, sunglasses, and safari hats. Jessica and Tim showed no sign of nervousness and everyone around them was far calmer than we are used to seeing minutes before show time. As family members were seated and the ceremony began, the tourists respectfully cleared out of the main area, and Jessica made her way down the aisle.

As she walked toward the altar with her father, I was firing away with my camera and thinking to myself how amazing this wedding would look in the pages of a magazine. It was only thirty seconds into the ceremony when the priest began to speak and I realized we weren't in North Carolina anymore. We were in Mexico, and the priest conducting the service was a life-long citizen of that country who happened to be proficient with the native tongue. We were in his country, in his church, and he was speaking his language.

In kindergarten, I learned to count to ten in Spanish. I can also say *please*, *thank you*, and *good day* in a fairly unconvincing accent. Beyond that, I'm pretty much reduced to taking English words and throwing whatever vowel sound that seems to fit to make the word sound "Spanishy." Earlier in the day, Meridith burst out laughing when I asked a cab diver, "How mucho?"

Thank goodness I was only there to take pictures, because I didn't understand a single word that the priest said. After a few moments of observation, I was relieved to see that no one else knew what he was saying either. The maid of honor had her head tilted to the side and brow furrowed into an expression that read, "When's he gonna start talking normal?"

Jessica and Tim could only stand there glancing at each other as the priest delivered his lengthy homily with dramatic and sweeping gestures. When he wanted them to do something or repeat something he would begin gesturing to help them understand what to do next. There was quite a game of international charades going on in front of me in that sanctuary. It was fun to watch, and I was relieved to see that everyone was taking it in stride and having fun. Aside from the fact that none of us in that church understood any of what had just been said or agreed to, the Mass proceeded flawlessly.

Because only close friends and family members were invited to the ceremony, there were maybe thirty people in attendance. The entire group barely filled up the first two rows of the church, which I would estimate easily had thirty or more rows of pews on either side of the aisle. When the ceremony began, I positioned myself halfway up the aisle. When the Mass was near the end, I turned around to set up at the end of the aisle for their exit. Mild shock and confusion confronted me as I saw that every available row behind me had been silently occupied during the course of the ceremony. Half of the church was packed full of people watching the end of this wedding! They weren't tourists this time, though; they were locals. No cargo shorts, or sunglasses, these folks were dressed for church, and I assumed they were waiting patiently for this wedding to end so they could get to some praying or confessing. I turned back around to face the ceremony in progress and composed the scene through my camera just before Jessica and Tim kissed. The priest then motioned for them to turn around and face the guests to be presented for the first time as husband and wife. They were married! Applause erupted from the first two rows, and a jubilant energy surrounded the couple as they made their way toward the back of the sanctuary. They didn't seem phased at all as they walked up the aisle through a crowd that was easily ten times larger than when Jessica first walked in.

Moments later, Meridith and I collected everyone and proceeded back inside the church to begin the traditional family group photos at the altar. We still had twenty minutes left in the block of time they had reserved, which was more than enough time. As we were going through the different family setups, more people flooded into the cathedral. We had no idea what was going on, but figured there was another Mass happening soon. As the crowd began to fill the remaining pews, we felt a lot of eyes watching us, creating a greater sense of urgency to wrap things up and not overstay our welcome.

We had only been shooting for less than ten minutes and were down to our last two groups when I felt a tap on my shoulder. I was trying hard to stay focused on getting the last shots done. I wanted to ignore the tap and keep plowing through, but it was the priest. Still in his vestments, I assumed that he was going to ask me if he could be in the next photo so that he could change out of the robe. I have found that one thing most presiders have in common is they want to get out of those hot and stuffy robes as quickly as they can. Instead, he said a few words in Spanish that I could not make out. Wanting to be respectful, I turned to him and leaned in a little closer, hoping that would somehow help me understand.

I thought I heard him say in slow and broken English, "Let... know when you es finish. They are...something, something... everybody."

I realized then that I really needed to become more internationally sophisticated, or at least learn basic Spanish beyond my trademark add a vowel to the end of every word method.

"The what for everybody?" I asked.

Ever patient, the priest motioned for me to look past him toward the back of the cathedral and said, "Need to bring body inside."

To this day, the image is still etched in my brain. When I looked past the priest, up the aisle and toward those mammoth twelve-foot doors that let the sunlight pour into the sanctuary, as my eyes adjusted to the brightness outside, I saw the silhouette of a square shape with people surrounding it. A split second later as my eyes adjusted more, I saw that there was a hearse backed up to the entrance and several men were getting ready to transport a casket through the very same doors and down the same aisle that Jessica had walked mere moments before. Everything from the last half-hour suddenly made sense.

I told the Priest that we were finished and would be moving along. Everyone in our group exited through the side door out into the courtyard where we began taking photos earlier during the baptism. As we assembled the final family group outside, I glanced around the wall of the courtyard in time to see six men carrying the casket up the steps and into the church. There was a packed house waiting for them. Just when one service ends, another begins.

I know that most Catholic churches schedule services back to back and on tight time lines, but this was one combination that we had never experienced before: baptism, wedding, and funeral with barely a breath between.

Jessica and Tim were married again a few hours later in a civil ceremony on a cliff overlooking the Pacific Ocean. As of publication, they are still living happily ever after. Such is the circle of life. You're born, you live, you love, you die, and if you are ever in downtown Puerto Vallarta, you might have a chance to see it all play out in the course of one afternoon.

Birds, Sex and Irrational Fear

I have a final phone conversation with my clients the week of their wedding to go over any last-minute details or talk through any photo requests or logistical challenges. It's basic stuff, like: "When should we meet you? Where will we meet you? Is the ceremony time you gave us nine months ago still accurate?"

Jenny planned for a low-key and casual ceremony on a pier in Wrightsville Beach, overlooking the ocean. She only had around thirty-five guests, making this an ideal beach location for a small wedding. The reception would take place at a well-known restaurant attached to the pier. Besides the convenience of the restaurant, having the ceremony on the pier avoided the most annoying thing about beach ceremonies for a photographer: tourists. On a public beach, random sunbathers and beach-goers can wander into the background of the ceremony photos. People are always milling about, completely unaware that a wedding is going on a few hundred feet away and that their Day-Glo orange cover-up will be the star of the show behind the wedding party. I told Jenny that the best thing about being on the pier was that we not only avoided background distractions, but this particular background was the best view on the beach—just pier, water, and sky. If there is a nicer view in that area for a wedding, I have yet to see it.

We began to discuss the timing of the ceremony when Jenny stopped herself mid-sentence and asked, "I know this is off topic, but do you know if there are a lot of seagulls around there?"

She asked me this because I grew up in the area and am familiar with the location, so she thought I would probably know. She also asked in a way that made me think that she might be concerned about the birds flying around during the ceremony, with a chance of seagull bombing raids on her and her guests.

In hopes of calming her fears I said, "Well, I've never seen a ton of seagulls around the pier. What you mostly see are the pigeons that hang out there. But they don't seem to fly around much. They just walk around on and under the pier."

Things got really quiet on the other end of the phone. "Pigeons? Are there really pigeons? I am completely and uncontrollably terrified of pigeons!" Her voice trembled.

At this point, realizing that I have stepped in a steaming pile of pigeon poo, I wanted to take my words back but knew that anything I said would make it worse. I tried earnestly to think of possible solutions and offer some miracle cure for her phobia, but I concluded that there was nothing I could say to ease her mind. So I decided to go with the lamest but easiest option: "I'm sure things will be just fine."

What was I going to say? It was the week of the wedding. She couldn't find another location in that time frame, and I didn't think there was any such thing as a pigeon trapper to make the birds go away. I hoped she would bring some meds to calm her down enough to not worry about a few birds ruining her wedding.

Accessory to Marriage

This would be a good time to mention that Jenny was not a freak, a drama queen, nor was she demanding of me. She never seemed that she would be bothered by much of anything. She and her fiancé Todd were two of the most fun and energetic people that we knew. As it turns out, the girl just didn't like birds.

On the wedding day, I arrived early to do a little location scouting and confirmed that the pigeons were indeed on the pier and congregating just a few feet from where Jenny would stand during her ceremony. The altar was set up next to a wooden gate that divided the pier into two halves. The half closest to the restaurant stood over the sandy beach and was typically used for outdoor dining. The half of the pier beyond the gate was closed to the public, making it a perfect sanctuary for the birds to live undisturbed, high above the beach, on several hundred feet of ocean-front property.

When I was growing up, this place was called Crystal Pier. It was a mile or so south of Johnny Mercer's, the only other commercial pier on Wrightsville Beach. Johnny Mercer's, with a souvenir store, video arcade, and bait and tackle shop, catered to tourists. Crystal Pier was known for its restaurant. Through the years, the names changed, but it was always a classy place for good seafood and a million-dollar view.

Sometimes people make decisions about their weddings for the sake of romantic intentions. Some decide that it's a good idea to get married in the dark, lit only by the soft glow of candlelight. Others think that a dreamy beach wedding is the way to go. There's nothing really wrong with either of those in theory. But the reality is that the photos produced in these situations are rarely as amazing as the vision that originated in the couple's imaginations. A German military strategist once noted, "No battle plan survives contact with the enemy."

Often the enemy is nature. I've seen many times where those little unforeseen elements of nature like wind, lighting, or mosquitoes turn a wedding day from fantasy into an unpleasant reality.

If you get married in the dark, the photos will not look as romantic as they will look dark. Thinking about the beach? Every day is windy as hell at the beach, and all the stuff that is brought out for the ceremony will get blown over. Your hair will be a wreck in less than five minutes, and at least one tiny grain of sand will most certainly find its way into the flower girl's eye causing a tearful distraction for everyone. If all of that sounds romantic, then go for it. Even so, when I find myself in these situations, I feel a great sense of responsibility to make the very most of the cards I have been dealt. That day, I was served gorgeous beach scenery with a side of pigeons.

Jenny was in an upbeat mood when she arrived, laughing and joking with her four bridesmaids. Since this was an intimate wedding with only a few dozen guests, I was working solo. I began by creating a few portraits of the bride and then worked on scenery shots while waiting for the guys to show up. Once Todd and his guys arrived, we were able to work with the whole wedding party on the beach. None of the typical Southern superstitions applied to this couple. So they chose to see each other before the wedding, and we were able to complete photos of the couple, families, and the wedding party before the ceremony. That was a good thing too, because I forgot to mention that it was also my son's third birthday, and Meridith expected me at the party by seven o'clock that evening.

The photo session before the guests arrived went better than expected. Ten minutes in, I was relieved that Jenny had not mentioned birds or displayed any phobic behavior. As I walked along the beach with the group, creating dramatically lit action shots, we arrived alongside the pier. I suggested that we walk underneath it because the other side had better light for portraits. Jenny wouldn't do it. She froze, her eyes darting nervously at the underside of the pier for any birds. She looked at me and said there was no way she would walk under there so some bird could swoop down on her.

"Maybe we can do it later," she said.

Oh, here we go, I thought. After several minutes, Todd talked her down off the ledge, and she eventually ducked down and ran fast under the pier. It's not that the pier was low and you had to duck; it probably had twenty feet or more of head clearance. But who knew what might come swooping down? So ducking and running seemed appropriate. We got to the other side and created lovely group portraits before everyone moved into the restaurant to prepare for the ceremony.

With about fifteen minutes before Jenny hit the aisle, I was back at the altar trying to come up with ways to make the pigeons go away. I had nothing. The little critters were used to people, so yelling or trying to wave them off had no effect. They felt safe on the other side of that gate and seemed to know that no one was going to come after them. Without doing something drastic that involved poison or a shotgun, I wasn't going to get those little buggers to move. I was resigned to the fact that this could be a complete meltdown or, at best, a huge distraction. But it wasn't my battle, so I decided to let it run its course.

The musicians began to play as the family was seated. Once Todd made his entrance and stood at the end of the aisle, Jenny appeared. She looked confident and happy as she walked toward Todd. I took my position and began shooting the ceremony. Up at the front I could see the pigeons walking around just a few feet away from Jenny and Todd on the other side of the gate. They were just inches away from the wedding party but seemed to be minding their own business. I was hoping that they wouldn't get spooked and take flight in the middle of the service. That would have been too much for Jenny to handle. She was already visibly distracted. As she stood there facing Todd, I saw her constantly glancing in the direction of the birds. Her hands trembled as she placed the ring on Todd's finger. I wondered if it was wedding-day nerves or pigeon-induced nerves. Throughout the fifteen-minute service, she looked at Todd with eyebrows raised in an expression that said, Get me out of here! So far she was keeping it together, though. If she could just hold on for a few more minutes, she'd be home free.

By the power vested in Tony, the minister for hire, Jenny and Todd were pronounced husband and wife and walked past me toward the crowd of ecstatic family and friends. Jenny looked especially excited, smiling and laughing the whole way back up the aisle. As always, there were hugs and congratulations.

When I caught up to the crowd, Jenny grabbed my shoulders and with a wild-eyed grin exclaimed, "I'm cured! Oh my God. I just saw pigeons having sex three feet away from me during my wedding! How can I be afraid of them now?"

While I'm sure that Jenny was truly happy to be married to Todd, it was clear that the highlight of her day was shattering her fear of pigeons by watching them get their freak on in the middle of her wedding. I guess sometimes it is okay to stand back and let people work things out themselves.

I'm with the Band

It probably doesn't surprise anyone to know that if it were not for alcohol, half of these stories would never have happened. One such tale of drunken excess happened at one of our favorite wedding venues. It's set on a farm complete with fields and cows. It even has a huge rustic barn just for events like wedding receptions. We had been photographing Nicole and Martin all day. Their formal obligations were complete and they were ready for a party. They informed me the week before their wedding that at ten o'clock when all of the older folks had gone home, the DJ was leaving and a friend's band was going to play until midnight.

At the reception, the guests had a splendid time mingling inside the barn. Just as planned, the elder guests and DJ split when the clock struck ten, and the band began to play. This really gave the party a second wind. See, no matter how experienced a photographer is, it's hard to create interesting images of people just milling about and talking. Action, motion, and energy are all necessary for creating dynamic reception imagery. So when the guests started dancing again it gave us so much more to work with.

There was one guest in particular who was just tearing up the dance floor. She was whipping her bright red hair in dramatic fashion and dancing with everyone—the guys, the girls, me (well, she tried but I wasn't having it). I guess the band was playing all her favorite songs. I had not noticed her earlier in the evening, but now she was the life of the party. Her enthusiastic flailing allowed us to capture some spectacular images full of color, motion, and energy—just the way we like. After a while, the band took a short break and the dance floor emptied as guests got more drinks and fresh air.

Meridith decided to take a break too, and when she returned from the ladies room she had a smirk on her face.

"What's that look about?" I asked.

"You know that red-headed girl you've been shooting like crazy? She's passed out cold on a sofa in the bathroom."

"She's just in there unconscious?"

"Well, there's another girl sitting on the end of the sofa like she's taking care of her."

I didn't think too much of it. It's not something we see every day, but certainly not the first time it's happened. Since I figured the girl's friend had things under control, it didn't seem necessary to begin sounding any alarm bells. Meridith, being the smarter of the two of us, decided it would be a good idea to at least let the event manager know what was happening. We found her in the kitchen and casually mentioned that one of the guests was out cold in the ladies room. We didn't expect her to flip out, but she did and blazed a trail to the ladies room. In hindsight, I could see that even though this place was a barn, it was still classy, and they probably didn't want folks passed out in their well-appointed facilities with the potential to redecorate it with the contents of their stomach. We moved on from that drama in progress and went back to work when the band started playing again. However, we knew with our star subject incapacitated there would not be much more to photograph.

About five minutes later, a half-dozen event staff rushed through the crowd on the dance floor toward the ladies room. Several of them looked panicked as they barked instructions into walkie-talkies. All of the commotion got Nicole's attention. She got up from her conversation on the other side of the room and walked over our direction.

"What's going on over there?" she asked.

Trying to play down the seriousness of the situation I said, "Oh, someone had a little too much from the bar and she's resting in the ladies room. I think the staff have it under control."

A wave of panic washed over her face as she darted to the rest room to see which one of her friends was in trouble.

Nicole reappeared in less than a minute. She was heading our direction again, but this time was different. Her lips were pressed tight and her brows were down. Oh crap, I thought. This girl was pissed and coming to give me a piece of her mind.

"Oh my God! I can't believe that stupid bitch is ruining my party! She's got like ten people back there shaking her trying to wake her up. I don't even know her, she's the lead singer's girlfriend!"

What was I going to say to that? We were in the last hour of the night, and the other 98 percent of the day had been flawless.

In an effort to appease Nicole, I simply said, "The staff here is great. They'll take care of this so that the rest of your guests will never know what happened."

That wasn't what Nicole wanted to hear. "She just came here to get drunk for free and have a party. No one invited her, but next thing I see she's throwing herself all over the place. If you have any pictures of her, you can delete them. I don't want to remember this."

That took the wind out of my sails. I had just spent the last forty-five minutes rocking some insane images of that girl having a great time. They were some of the most interesting photos of the night, but I was told they did not matter. That was tough to hear, but there was no saving the situation. Nicole thanked us for the day, gave me a big hug, and said that we could leave if we wanted. She said there was nothing else going on that night that she would want photographed.

Meridith and I packed up our gear, and as we pulled out of the parking lot to head home, an ambulance drove up with lights flashing. It turned out that after shaking, slapping, and splashing water on the poor girl, no one could wake her up, and they had to call in the professionals. So much for the other guests not finding out. Nicole was right though. Flashing ambulance lights and EMTs wheeling a gurney through the reception would not make for good memories in a wedding album!

Most Memorable Quotes Ever

"I need you to put these eye drops in her drink. It will give her massive diarrhea so she can't be at my wedding tomorrow."

The bride at the rehearsal dinner instructing the wedding planner about one of the groom's guests. The request was denied.

OMG! It's Dad!

It is a joy to witness people's excitement when they think they have experienced something miraculous. Ella was married in an outdoor ceremony at her parents' home. We had photographed her older sister's wedding a few years earlier. The whole family was warm and gracious, and I remember thinking back then that Ella was gorgeous, and I hoped we'd get to be at her wedding someday.

So there we were, another beautiful May afternoon. This time, Ella was in the wedding dress and her sister Maria was the matron of honor. The ceremony was complete and we were halfway through the formal family groups. We always try to get through these photos swiftly because, let's face it, at that point in the day people are ready for a drink and a party. It's the most frantic part of the schedule for us because, while our goal is to corral large groups of people and get them all looking in the same direction with pleasant smiles on their faces, the guests' goal usually involves finding the bar and getting a buzz on. I breezed through the groups with Ella's family, and it was time for Richard's family photos. Everyone was cooperating so far, and I was shooting away to get the list complete.

If you read the previous sections about Uncle Bobs and Aunt Sallies, then you know that we sometimes have quite a camera crew beside us during the formal portraits. This day was no exception. As I photographed Richard's family, there were at least three people on either side of me with their snappy cams firing away. They always ask me if their flash is going to ruin my photos. I think to myself, Your flash doesn't, but it certainly does mess things up when you repeatedly ask the folks in front of me to look at you as I'm tying to photograph them. Happy snappers can make simple things take a lot longer sometimes.

I was in the middle of photographing a group when I noticed one of the snappers on my right look down at her camera and gasp, "Oh my G…"

It was Richard's sister. Her eyes were wide with surprise, and she was visibly shaken. Still focused on wrapping up the last few groups, I didn't pay close attention or try to figure out what made her react the way she did. She rushed over to a group of her family and began passing the camera around for everyone to see the image on the back. A moment later, a dozen people huddled around this girl and her camera. I remember wondering what could possibly be so special about a picture of four people standing beside each other to warrant gasps and visible emotion.

As I wrapped up the family photos, what really baffled me was that she never returned to take more pictures. If they were that insanely great, then why wouldn't she want more pictures with other people in them? It was as if she got her one masterpiece for the day and was off to find a wall in a museum on which to hang it. I asked Meridith if she knew what that was all about. She said that she overheard most of what happened in the huddle, but it was a long story that she would tell me later.

Halfway through the reception, after everyone had eaten and the party was getting under way, I asked Meridith to tell me what happened earlier with Richard's sister.

"Oh yeah, I couldn't tell you before because you would have burst out laughing. When you had Richard's mom and grandmother lined up around him, his sister was taking pictures when she saw one on the camera that caught her eye. It had a green circle of light that was right beside Richard's mom. She ran over to her family and exclaimed, 'It's Daddy! Look, right there, that's an orb! See that green circle of light? I've seen that on TV. That's how the spirits travel around. That's Daddy in the picture! Isn't that amazing? It's a miracle!'"

I admit I laughed, perhaps a bit hysterically. Of all the things I could have imagined happening, that was nowhere on the list.

"She was serious?" I asked Meridith.

"I'm telling you, James, the poor girl was shaking and had tears in her eyes. As far as she was concerned, her father made a trip from the spirit world to visit her brother's wedding. That's why I didn't want to say anything to ruin her moment."

It sounded like one of those ghost-hunter reality shows on the Sci-fi Channel. Richard's father had passed away several years earlier and, while I'm sure he was there in spirit, the green "orb" had a less than supernatural explanation.

It's a photographic occurrence called flare, and it's what happens when sunlight hits the camera lens and bounces around between the glass elements inside the camera. Sometimes it shows up green; other times it's blue. It's usually round or octagonal and appears in a photo as one or several circles of various sizes, depending on the type of camera. If you've ever watched Kung Fu Theater on TV, or even old western movies, you've probably seen it. Some professional photographers incorporate flare circles intentionally into their images for trendy effect. I can see where someone might find this phenomenon of physics out of the ordinary. But other-worldly? That stretches my brain too far.

I would never tell Richard's sister about flare and I hope she never reads this book. On her brother's wedding day, she knew without a doubt that she had captured a piece of the great beyond. The look on her face at seeing what she knew was her deceased father being present in spirit was an expression of child-like wonder. It was the same look that my kids have when they talk about the tooth fairy, the Easter bunny, or Santa Claus, all of whom are also totally real to the children.

Wedding Crashers

You would think that people would have a little more respect than to show up at a party uninvited. But we see wedding crashers all the time. It's usually obvious when underdressed people stick their heads inside a ballroom to peek inside. I would classify those people as insensitive onlookers. Most are just gawking at the decorations, some are enjoying the music, while the bold ones help themselves to a beer or two from the bar. Real crashers, on the other hand, are harder to spot and sometimes no one knows about them until after the fact. Sometimes the people we later find out were crashers were having the most fun on the dance floor, and we have lots of pictures of them.

I had a couple come into our office to pick up their post-wedding products and view their wedding day images for the first time. They were snuggled up nice and comfy on the sofa in our gallery looking at their images projected on the wall. We heard the usual oohs, aahs, and the occasional, "Wow, I never saw that!"

When we came to the dancing part of the reception, Heather and Corey burst out laughing, pointed and said, "There they are!"

"Huh, there's who? Did I do something wrong? Did I do something great? Somebody clue me in."

Heather explained that the woman in the yellow dress, whom we had just seen dancing with her father, her uncle, and Corey's brother, was a crasher. She and her friend in the black and gold dress were tearing up the dance floor for about an hour, and I remember them being a major source of amusement for several older gentlemen in the crowd. Everyone on Heather's side assumed they were friends of Corey's, and everyone on Corey's side thought they were with Heather's people. They looked to be the same age as the rest of the wedding party, so they fit in seamlessly and were having a great time getting the real wedding guests to dance. They made it possible for us to create some exciting photographs.

Since Heather and Corey weren't on the dance floor at the time, they didn't know about these two until they caught up with some of their friends after the honeymoon and started to compare stories from the day. Seeing the photos made it real for them and luckily they have a really good sense of humor about it.

Looking at the expressions on her dad's face dancing with with yellow dress girl, Heather said, "Hell, they might have crashed my wedding, but look at his face. You can't even buy entertainment like that."

There are times when crashers are more conspicuous, but no one cares because they bring a welcome shot of energy to a reception. There was one year when Halloween fell on a Saturday and we were shooting a wedding in downtown Wilmington, North Carolina. We were in a great old renovated building on Front Street that just two years earlier had been Roudabushes seed store. Front Street is the main drag of downtown Wilmington nightlife, and it was teaming with throngs of people out barhopping to celebrate Halloween.

While dinner took place upstairs, the dancing and party portion of the reception happened at street level. Large windows allowed us to see all the creeps and freaks in costume walking by and sometimes looking in on us to see the party in progress. This was not a Halloween-themed wedding; it was simply the only day left in October that St. Mary's Church was available. We tried to maintain normality with drunken people in costumes outside and equally drunken people in wedding attire inside.

It wasn't long before the smokers among the guests went outside to light up. Three or four of them struck up a conversation with a group of college guys who were dressed up as Transformers, the robots in disguise that turn into jets, trucks, and other things to fight for dominance of the planet. Their costumes were homemade from cardboard boxes, pipes, tubes, and aluminum foil. They were well painted and detailed. These guests thought it would be a great idea to invite the robots inside to liven up the dance floor for a few minutes. It took some convincing, but the three guests had a good buzz going and wouldn't take no for an answer. Next thing we knew, there were a half-dozen seven-foot-tall robots on the dance floor with the bride and the wedding party.

Everyone went nuts. People loved it. The band tried a version of "Mr. Roboto." We got photos of Grandma dancing with Optimus Prime. The best part is that the robo-patrol didn't wear out their welcome. They danced and entertained the crowd for about ten minutes and then were gone. Even though we have no idea who they were, those party people will not soon forget the time their friend's wedding was invaded by robots.

There are other times when the crashers are professional thieves. I know you're saying to yourself, "No way, that only happens on TV." But it's true. If you're a dedicated crasher, weddings are a great place to score more than just some free drinks or an easy groomsman. There's a lot of loot sitting on that gift table, and it's rarely guarded or even monitored.

A few days after returning home from a fantastic wedding in Charleston, South Carolina, I received a phone call from the bride's mother.

"I'm sure you got some lovely photos on Saturday," she said. "And I can't wait to see them. Unfortunately, I need to see if you can look through them for two women who crashed the wedding and stole several of the gifts."

"Wow, really?" I asked. "How did that happen?"

She recounted that two women in their early twenties, one wearing a green dress, the other in a black and white dress, snuck into the reception, ate dinner, danced, and then left, each with arms full of gifts. There were hundreds, possibly thousands of dollars of gifts missing. All of the cards that had either cash or checks for the couple were gone too. She confided that her daughter Allie (the bride) was extremely upset over this because it put them in an embarrassing situation: they had to call each guest they didn't have a gift from and ask them if they brought one or not. If they did, then they needed an approximate value to add to the police report. I felt really bad for them. These were polite Southern people, and the predicament they were in was highly uncivilized.

She wanted me to search our photos from the dance floor to see if any might help the police. The suspects' descriptions fit about a half-dozen guests who were on the dance floor at any given time during the evening. She went on to explain that a few of her friends saw the two girls dancing it up around ten p.m. But people thought they were friends of the groom so no one mentioned it. Later that evening, a different group of people saw these same girls leaving with bags and boxes, assuming they were the wedding planner's assistants helping to load up the car.

The crazy part was this was not only the nicest, but also the most secure venue in Charleston. It had a nine-foot brick wall surrounding the entire property, and the only way in or out was to pass by the security guards posted at each of the two gates. Apparently these girls knew how to fool them too. They never aroused suspicion until nearly half of the gifts were missing.

When all pieces of the story came together it appeared that these two ladies were quite skilled at crashing parties and taking off with the valuables. On top of that, they seemed comfortable with getting their party on and mixing with the guests before they got away with the loot. The Charleston Police Department had three similar reports from recent weddings with the same descriptions and modus operandi.

I launched a full-scale FBI-level investigation in my office that morning. Pouring through the thousands of images we took that day, zooming into backgrounds, hoping to catch a glimpse of something that could be of any use to the police. Would I be the one who could help the cops crack the case and bust the perps? I hoped so. I was so into this, going image by image, excited and determined to do my part for justice. My eyes were fixated on the screen and hurting because I kept forgetting to blink. My pulse quickened as I got to the dancing images. As the theme song from "Dragnet" played on my computer, I saw the first green dress.

Ah-ha! I thought. Gotcha, bitches! Wait, no, I think that's Allie's friend from college. I'm pretty sure that girl was in the room where the bridesmaids got ready.

A few images later there was the black and white dress. Yes! Oh, wait, she's definitely not in her twenties. Crap, where were those girls?

I wasn't fazed though, because I knew that between both Meridith and myself shooting that entire evening, I was bound to strike gold soon enough. Besides, the entire *Ultra-Lounge: The Crime Scene* album was loaded up, and I had at least forty minutes of theme music to keep me inspired. I tagged every single image that included anyone in green or black or white. Just as the "Mission: Impossible" theme hit its stride, I came to the end of my collection of photos. I had three totally useless images. There were no faces, and these girls only appeared in the backgrounds. The best I had was a dancing shot that showed half of the girl in the green dress, with the other in the background, turned away from the camera. How did they do that? How were they right in front of us yet still managed to avoid us? They must really be good at what they do.

If they truly run this scam every week or so, I can only imagine that if you go to either of these ladies' apartments you will find a lot of kick-ass kitchen accessories and a large assortment of fine china that doesn't match. They never did catch those wedding-bash bandits. If you're ever in Charleston and an attractive young lady tries to sell you a brand new Crock-pot out of the back of her car, call the sheriff.

Oh No, She Didn't!

There are enough unspoken rules and traditions in Southern weddings to fill a small library. This makes it inevitable that at least a few guests will commit a breach of proper etiquette. Some infractions are innocent enough. If you grew up in New Jersey, we can't expect you to understand why Southern people love pictures of brides on staircases or in front of gazebos. We don't assume that you'll like sweet tea, but you really should try it once before telling us about how you do things back home. There are a few areas of Southern-wedding etiquette that simply cannot be ignored. To dismiss these rules is an affront to Southern sensibilities and is considered another intolerable act of Northern aggression.

Sarah and Matthew's August wedding day at Wrightsville Beach was downright balmy, not the usual 100 percent humidity. Meridith and I were excited to be shooting a wedding in our hometown for a change. Sarah and her sisters were Southern, proper, stylish, and fun. These three beautiful women, relatively close in age, showed the all-for-one-and-one-for-all attitude you see in sisters who are close.

Mary Kate was the middle child and she went through the day making sure that everything was taken care of for Sarah. Keeping

James D. Walters

her hydrated, carrying her lip-gloss, and even assisting with trips to the lady's room, Mary Kate was a trooper. She was fun-loving, but serious about her duties as her sister's maid of honor. At the reception, when the time came for the toast, Mary Kate delivered a heartfelt tribute to Sarah and her new brother-in-law, Matthew. It was the best kind of toast: sincere, from the heart, but brief and to the point. I let my mind wander and thought about someday working with Mary Kate on her wedding. What a great bride she would be to photograph.

The toasts ended and the party continued with dancing and lively conversation in every corner of the Surf Club. Friends and family caught up with each other and reminisced about the old days. Sarah was near the dance floor when the DJ cranked up that familiar Cindy Lauper tune and announced, "It is now time for the bouquet toss! All single ladies to the dance floor, please." After a quick scramble to find the tossing bouquet, Sarah took her place at the front edge of the dance floor, and the single ladies assembled behind her.

It was the time in the evening when all the polite events had taken place, and things were getting real. The civilized dances and the cake-cutting were just fuzzy memories and the girls in the room were ready for action. The high heels were off and tossed around the perimeter of the dance floor for me to break an ankle. The hair was up in a ponytail courtesy of a black hair band worn on each girl's wrist all day. These single ladies had a fire in their eyes. The bouquet toss was their time to shine.

Sarah was in position and ready to toss. She looked back at the crowd of eager women standing behind her, locked eyes with Mary Kate, and gave her a wink and a nod signaling that those flowers would be headed her direction.

The DJ signaled to me asking if I wanted to do a fake toss first. I shook my head and said "No, let's do this."

He gave the girls ample instructions about no pushing, shoving, biting, hair pulling, scratching, or punching. Some DJs love giving that spiel. It adds drama for the crowd and positions the bouquet as a prize that should be won by any means necessary. The girls in the front row are always the serious ones. They're crouched slightly with arms spread to the side, as if they are holding back the rest of the group or about to spring into a killer kung fu move to score that bouquet. Mary Kate was front and center, and she meant business. Her boyfriend was there at the wedding, but there was no ring on her finger yet. Catching this clutch of flowers could change everything.

"Okay, ready Sarah?" asked the DJ. "Here we go ladies, one-two-three!"

Sarah threw the bouquet behind her with everything she had. My camera focused on her and, as I was firing away, I caught bits of the action through the viewfinder between shots. I saw the flowers leave Sara's hands, then the camera shutter opened, obscuring my view for a split second. Next I saw Mary Kate's eyes look upward as she was beginning to jump, then another shutter cycle. The third image I didn't understand because, while Mary Kate's hands were clasped together, they were completely empty and the bouquet was nowhere to be seen. While I focused on Sarah during all of this, Meridith focused on the group of girls, and her photos showed a totally different perspective. First image, girls poised to jump; second image, the whole group in motion, their feet off the floor with the bouquet just inches away from Mary Kate's outstretched fingers. The third image showed the blurred figure of a girl moving swiftly from the sidelines, running out in front of the group, and snagging the bouquet just before it reached Mary Kate. Meridith's fourth photo showed a visibly furious Mary Kate looking off in the direction of the bouquet dasher, who was on the other side of the room laughing and enjoying her accomplishment. Sarah looked back to confirm that the bouquet reached its intended target, only to see her little sister throwing a good old-fashioned hissy fit.

"Who the hell is that bitch?" Mary Kate yelled.

Tactically, it was a very clever plan. The victorious bouquet catcher used the advantage of surprise and speed to out maneuver her competition and claim the prize. In the pecking order of single ladies, however, this girl had screwed up royally. Perhaps no one told her that it is a Southern law that if the bride has a sister who is eligible to be married, then she is the one who catches the bouquet. There is no forgiveness for those who disregard this code of conduct. This isn't one of those frivolous laws like coming to a full and complete stop when you approach a stop sign. She broke a serious law. The kind you just don't challenge—like the law of gravity, or that one that says not to wear a black belt with brown shoes. All the girls can get together out there on that dance floor and it's fun to think that you might be the one to walk away with the flowers. If you have any sense, though, you'll step to the side if that thing sails through the air in your direction, and you'll let the bride's sister have her moment. The end. No exceptions, no excuses.

The next thing I saw was Mary Kate all up in that girl's personal space. It was obvious that they didn't know each other because Mary Kate was venting her rage and giving it to the flower thief with both barrels. From across the room, I could only read their body language. From Mary Kate's frantic gesturing and the other girl's perplexed expression, it was obvious that the thrill of victory was quickly fading for the once-proud flower catcher. She stood there stunned while Mary Kate yelled and flailed her arms, repeatedly pointing at the flowers. It was obvious that the girl was still trying to figure out what she had done wrong. At one point, she pushed the flowers toward Mary Kate as a peace offering. That only made Mary Kate more indignant; she grabbed a handful of petals from the top and threw them to the floor in disgust.

When it looked like a girl fight was imminent, Mary Kate's friends moved in. They pulled her back onto the dance floor and got her a few more drinks to calm her down. The girl from the sidelines turned out to be one of Matthew's cousins from Maryland. Poor girl, I'm sure she had innocent visions of catching a bouquet at a wedding and having a great story to tell everyone at work on Monday. Instead she got herself a heapin' helpin' of Southern-girl scorn.

Behind the Scenes Insight

How to Drive the Wedding Photographer Crazy

There are certain things that happen at weddings that either make life difficult for us photographers or prevent us from doing our job. Like the limo driver getting lost or Aunt Sally getting in our way, while things like drunk people with sparklers that jeopardize our personal safety make us cringe. Sometimes though, we encounter behavior that is just highly annoying or embarrassing. The following list includes a few of the things my fellow wedding photographers and I whine about most when we get together. One or more of these happen at nearly every wedding. Like many creative folks, photographers have a vision of how things should be, and when reality fails to match that vision (which is about 99.9 percent of the time), we tend to whine about it. We're not proud of that whining, but admitting it is half the battle on the road to recovery.

1. **DJ Karaoke**—When the DJ sings along on the microphone to the parts of the song he knows, or even if he doesn't know some of the words. It's totally okay to mumble along to that Def Leopard song. Who's really listening, right? I'm not sure why, but this happens a lot more often at the coast than any other location. We see it at the laid-back sorts of affairs where the groom's uncle is most likely to show up in a Hawaiian shirt and sandals, chewing on a drinking straw while everyone else is in a suit and tie.

2. **Parents, shut up!**—It never fails. I will be in the process of creating the most incredible candid portrait of a little kid who is just being his or her adorable little self and unaware of me. If Mom notices what I'm doing, she instinctively tries to be helpful and yells at the kid, "Smile at the man with the camera!" It kills my shot every time and makes me want to choke the parent.

3. **Break Dancing**—Women will abandon their high heels around the edge of the dance floor for me and everyone else to twist their ankles on for the remainder of the evening. Sometimes I think about how fun it would be to take all of those discarded shoes and hide them around the ballroom. It would be a most entertaining treasure hunt later in the evening. Lucky for everyone, I don't act on my daydreams very often.

4. **Intoxicated Guests with Sparklers—** Horrifying. Need I say more?

5. **The idiot who starts chanting, "One more song, one more song, one more song..."**—It was the last song. The bandleader said so before he started and gave you three minutes to come to terms with the inevitable fact that the party must end at some point. It's over, go home, sober up, and party again another day.

6. **People who ask, Where do I stand for the picture?**—If you are not standing in a spot that will make for a nice group photo, I promise I'll let you know and then guide you gently through the process of correcting the issue. There is no need to be the squeaky wheel and call attention to the fact that I have not yet personally addressed your specific position in this photo. Chill out Grandma Diva!

7. **Clueless Best Men** who act like they didn't know they would have to give a toast. Seriously? Is their Internet broken? The worst part is how they feign surprise when handed the microphone, so upon delivering their hastily prepared speech, guests are not surprised to hear a series of platitudes that are incoherent and painfully craptastic.

8. **Clever Maids or Matrons of Honor** who give their toast in the form of a cutesy poem they wrote the night before on the hotel notepad. It's a guaranteed recipe for horrible pacing with juvenile sounding rhymes full of puns, inside jokes, and clichés. It should be avoided at all costs. It takes a lot of energy to stay creative all day and produce great photos. It takes equal amounts of energy to restrain myself from rolling my eyes whenever I hear one of these toasts.

9. **Bellyaching Bridesmaids** who just won't shut up about it being cold or hot or windy or that it might rain sometime that day. Quit your bitchin'! Let your girl enjoy her day and stop bringing everyone down. Yes, it's hot. She chose to get married in August; don't rub it in. If you don't change your attitude, I'm going to keep photographing you on your side with the lazy eye!

10. **Whack Wedding Directors** who flip their wig if any guest sees the bride before the ceremony. Really, no one will turn to a pillar of salt for seeing her from 100 yards away. If the bride doesn't mind, then don't make her think she should.

11. **Photographers** who complain about every little thing that doesn't go their way or isn't perfect. Good grief, they're annoying. Oh, wait…

Most Memorable Quotes Ever

"A good toast is like a woman's skirt: long enough to cover the subject but short enough to hold our interest."

Best man's speech, adapted
from a quote by Ronald Knox
(1888-1957)

Chapter 5
The Darndest Thing Happened

The minute I think I have seen and heard it all when it comes to wedding related insanity, someone is quick to tell me his or her own crazy experience. Whenever I get together with other wedding professionals like planners, caterers, florists, and, of course, other photographers, I can be sure that war stories of our most unbelievable experiences will be exchanged over cocktails. There are the stories of outrageousness you might expect, like a bride starting a fight with her groom at the reception and one of them leaves in an ambulance instead of the Bentley. Others take a more bizarre angle; a friend told me about a bride who disclosed to him that she was selling her eggs to a fertility clinic in order to pay for the photography deposit.

Nearly everyone in this industry tells stories that are so outrageous and hard to believe you might think they are lies. Once you've experienced a few unbelievable events of your own, however, you begin to realize that truth really is stranger than fiction.

Many of the stories in other parts of this book happened because of people who acted outrageously. The stories in this chapter are about places and circumstances that seem to attract the element of uncertainty through no obvious provocation on our part.

Crack in the Sidewalk

A beautiful April day put Meridith and me in historic Savannah, Georgia. We absolutely love that town. It has tons of historic architecture and moss-covered oaks most everywhere you look. While it's a true and proper Southern town, it also possesses a quirky vibe that makes it more approachable and lets you know that it doesn't take itself too seriously.

Early in the day, I was full of excitement about the wedding and was ready to give it all of my best energy. We typically arrive at a ceremony earlier than necessary to check things out. Since this was a destination wedding for us, we stayed in a hotel the night before and got to the location extra early to scout the most attractive angles and scenes for taking photos later that day.

After years of visits to Savannah, walking around its historic squares and being enchanted by its beauty, I was thrilled to photograph a wedding there. I felt like I had finally made it big. They don't even know what's about to hit them, I thought to myself. I'm gonna throw every kind of awesome idea I have at these people, and when they see their pictures, they will love them so much they'll cry.

I had high hopes for the day. But experience has taught me to listen to that inner voice a little more carefully and throttle those high hopes down to more realistic levels.

I don't remember much about the bride or groom that day. I can't recall their names, but I'm pretty sure she was blonde and he was, well, there. There's a good reason for this lack of memory, though: they hired us through a planner and wanted no direct communication with us. When we did finally meet them, they let us know that they "really weren't into photos." According to the planner, they just wanted "Good photographers who would cover all the bases for our parents." Great! So once I knew that the couple didn't really care about us or the value we would bring to their wedding, then I could move on with forgetting about them as people and focus on being super excited about shooting a wedding in Savannah!

Three hours before the wedding, Meridith and I walked around the church and Telfair Square. The wedding was at Telfair-freaking-Square! I could barely contain myself. If you ever read anything about Savannah, there's a good chance it will mention this place. The history and architecture in this little area alone were enough to fill me full of inspiration and make me lose my cool. I instantly become a giddy tourist taking pictures of doorknobs and shutters and church spires.

Accessory to Marriage

As we walked around the square and discussed photo possibilities, I looked ahead of us and spotted money! I can be kind of a dork like that when I find a penny or a quarter on the sidewalk. My inner child surfaces and I hold up my prize and shout "*Woo-Hoo!*" This was different, though.

It was the mother-load, actual paper money! I couldn't tell how much, because it was folded up really small and seemed to be wedged into a crack in the old brick sidewalk. It was one of those larger cracks caused when an old tree is desperately trying to grow beside the sidewalk and the roots push the bricks upward. I bent down, worked it out of the crevice, and began to unfold the bill.

"Score! It's five bucks!"

As I continued to unfold the bill, I realized that it was so much more than just five dollars, because sitting in the middle of old Abe Lincoln's face were a bunch of little white rocks. Now I'm about as gangsta as any other suburban, middle-aged white guy. All of my formal gangsta training came from watching "Yo! MTV Raps" back in the 1980s. Those were the days when rappers like Snoop Dog and Dr. Dre mainly rhymed about smokin' weed, poppin' caps, and hittin' bitches. It was good times, but it didn't prepare me for this situation.

I thought to myself, "I've seen Dateline and 20/20. This stuff is drugs, probably crack! Some dude rolled it up in this five-dollar bill, stuffed it in the sidewalk, and told some other dude where to find it. Right now, somewhere close by there's a crackhead who's going to show up to no crack in the sidewalk and be pissed!"

At that point, I was a paranoid wreck, and I suddenly saw the city I loved in a whole new way. Immediately my head went up and darted side to side as I scanned the area for anything suspicious, like people hanging around across the street, or those white unmarked vans popular with kidnappers. My paranoia started messing with me, and everyone around became the object of my suspicion. I envisioned the lady you might see in the gangster movie, happily strolling with what you think is a baby. But as she passes you (in slow motion of course) a little person raises up from the stroller and fills you full of lead! Ten thousand scenarios like that flowed through my mind. None of them ended happily.

What if the crackhead saw me pick it up? With *New Jack City* being the only drug movie I had ever seen, I was convinced that any moment four thugs in a beat up Chevy Caprice would chase me through town until we got to the Savannah River bridge, where they would try to throw me off. Then, as I hung there over the edge, grasping the railing for dear life, they would saw off my hand and send me to a watery end.

"Freakin' crap!" I thought. "What if it's not thugs at all? What if this is some kind of police sting operation and I'm on a surveillance camera and about to get busted for taking the bait. I don't have time to go downtown and get booked. I'm too pretty to go to jail. But more importantly, I've got a wedding to shoot in a few hours. How will I explain how I came into possession of a crack-tainted fiver?"

Within about twenty seconds, the excitement of finding five bucks turned to disbelief over the predicament my imagination was creating. Despite all of that, there was no way I was throwing the money back down on the ground. I'm not wired that way. I let the rocks spill onto the sidewalk, and we kept walking behind the church. I scraped the bill down the side of the wall to get as much of the "residue" off as possible.

Soon, the realization hit that I had crack residue on my hands. Damn it! There were traces of it on the money, and surely it was now in my pants pocket too. All I needed was one of the police patrols around the square to get close enough with a drug-sniffing dog, and it would be all over for me. In my mind, this five-dollar bill was taking me places I'd never been before, and I didn't even have to light it up! Once the church was opened, I spent much longer than probably necessary washing my hands, using plenty of soap between each finger, and even under the nails for good measure. I had to find calm and refocus my attention to the wedding.

The rest of my day was spent within a hundred yards of that spot. Carrying the five-dollar bill in my pocket, I was distracted by the urge to constantly look over my shoulder, wondering if there would be a guy bent down searching for something among the bricks. I never saw anyone, but then again I was a little preoccupied with the twenty-six person wedding party, which I was trying to keep in one spot long enough for pictures.

I think we ended up using the five dollars to pay for the parking deck. It was by far the most stressful money I've ever made.

Wardrobe Malfunction

It's a magical moment when a bride reaches the top of the steps and stands at the foot of the famous aisle at the Duke University Chapel. She may have been there dozens of times before, but this time she feels small standing beneath the neo-Gothic arches which rise to seventy-three feet above. Standing there for what seems like a blink of an eye while her dress and veil are adjusted, she reminds herself to take in the moment. As the organ grows louder, she strains to see the expression of her future husband nearly three hundred feet away. The crescendo builds. She takes her father's extended arm, and the guests rise and look her direction. The vibrations of the organ pipes right above her head are felt through her body, overwhelming her senses and helping to extinguish her nervousness. She takes a deep breath and then that first step. For most brides, the first step is just like the second, and the third. Each one is progressively easier until several hundred steps later she has arrived to begin a new phase of her life.

I was standing behind Avery and her father as they experienced that unforgettable moment for themselves. Inside my camera was a breathtaking composition of their silhouettes standing before a beautifully lit masterpiece of architecture. For Avery, that first step was magical. Unfortunately, the second step included a pause and then a stumble. Frantic, the wedding director leaned in to ask what was wrong. Was it nerves? Did she twist her ankle? Avery looked confused and I saw a lot of head shaking and pointing down at the dress. I heard Avery say she was caught on something and would fall if she took another step.

There we all were in the middle of a mysterious mini-crisis. Luckily for Brooke, the wedding director, the train of Avery's dress was huge. Brooke easily hid herself as she crouched down and lifted the dress to see what was wrong. It appeared that whatever snaps or straps had been supporting Avery's crinoline earlier had given up and were no longer doing the job. Avery had stepped on the front of her crinoline and was now caught up in it.

If you're a guy, you might be saying, "Um, what's this crinoline thing you speak of?" Don't be afraid. A crinoline is an undergarment made of several layers of stiff fabric. It's worn underneath the dress and is used to fluff out the sides. It takes a gown from normal to princess-worthy. They are sometimes called petticoats and are often held to the waist by a simple string or ribbon.

Once Brooke determined what was wrong, she didn't miss a beat and ordered Avery in a very firm but gentle tone to "Step high and keep walking!" Still looking straight ahead as if nothing was wrong, Avery did as instructed with perfect calm and flawless execution. She stepped right out of the rest of the crinoline and smoothly down the aisle. Brooke, still hidden from view behind Avery and her father, held onto the back of the crinoline. Once it was fully out from under the dress, she tossed it backward with one sweeping motion past me, out the door and down the stairs behind us, like a bullfighter tossing the red cape after slaying his opponent. With all eyes now on Avery, Brooke looked back at the crinoline lying at the bottom of the stairs out of the guests' view. Knowing that she had just saved the day, she gave a celebratory fist pump with a barely audible, "Yes!" She walked away proud.

The guests didn't see a thing. They just wondered why it took so long for Avery to get going. Brooke's quick thinking turned a potential disaster into a minor inconvenience.

Most Memorable Quotes Ever

"I'm from out of town. Where do you go to buy drugs around here?"

Asked by a drunk guest at the end of the evening.

Run!

Moore Square in downtown Raleigh can be beautiful and scary at the same time. There are great wedding venues and churches within walking distance, and the square itself offers the potential of natural-looking backgrounds in the midst of an urban area. It is also beside the city's main bus terminal and just a block or two from a methadone clinic and a homeless shelter. It's the place downtown where you are most likely to find people sleeping on benches in the middle of the day in every season. If you are walking by or through the square, panhandlers will seek you out to ask for money.

One warm September day, Meridith and I had just finished a ceremony at a church a few blocks around the corner from the square. The bride, Diane, requested that we visit a few locations downtown with her entire wedding party for some fun, less formal photos to compliment the ones we took at her church earlier. We took the whole group a block over from Moore Square, walked around for a bit, and created several memorable images. Once we finished, the couple rode away in a classic Bentley and Meridith and I began the walk back to our car to drive a few more blocks to the reception.

When we arrived downtown earlier, the only parking spot available was on the side of the square farthest from where we wanted to photograph the wedding party. It's a place where you look over your shoulder a lot and you feel vulnerable, especially when your arms are full carrying thousands of dollars of photo and lighting equipment. Meridith and I walked briskly back to our car when we noticed a guy approaching us with that familiar, inquiring look.

He was about twenty feet away when he shouted, "Hey, can I axe y'all a question?"

"Damn it!" I thought. "I don't even know what he's going to axe me, but I'm sure my lame attempt to get him to go away will sound stupid."

I started to open my mouth to humor the guy when Meridith decided she would just nip this in the bud. She put her hand up and said, "No."

Oh, shit. She's about to get us killed, I thought to myself.

After hearing no and getting the hand from Meridith, this guy was visibly pissed. He started coming closer, walking along side us with an aggressive strut, arms flailing, fingers pointing, cursing, and yelling at us about how we were terrible human beings.

"Oh, y'all just think y'all better than people! Can't axed no questions 'cause y'all's too good. Well, fuck y'all! Fuck bofa y'all!"

As he got even closer, we didn't wait to hear the rest. We hauled ass across that square toward the car as fast as we could. It was broad daylight and there were plenty of other people around, but none of that matters when you feel like you are about to get a beat down by a dude in a park. All I remember is the metal light stand I was carrying on my shoulder clang, clang, clanging right beside my ear with every stride, and the bag slung over my shoulder was knocking against my hip as I tried to keep the lenses from falling out while running in dress shoes.

We made it to the car, tossed the gear inside, jumped in, and locked the doors. We were out of breath and halfway between freaked out and laughing about the whole thing. I pulled out of the parking space and was only able to move twenty feet before having to stop for a red light. Immediately in front of us, in the middle of the street, was our guy again. Waving his arms, yelling at the top of his lungs, and generally making a spectacle of himself. There was nowhere we could go. All we could do is stare straight ahead and keep repeating to ourselves, "This isn't really happening."

Thank God the light finally turned green because I was afraid the guy was going to start throwing things at the car. Instead, he decided to stand in front of it and block us from leaving. He was having fun with us now. I couldn't go left or right without running over this idiot and him trying to sue for some bogus injury. Meridith was beginning to panic again as she dialed 911.

I thought about how I would explain to Diane why we missed the introductions and first dances at her reception. "Well Diane, you know that crazy Moore Square and those folks with their shenanigans." That sounded stupid. Lucky for us, our human roadblock either got bored or saw a cop and, after about a minute, headed off in the direction of the square.

We got to the reception in time to see that the bride and groom's Bentley had broken down a block from the venue, and the groom was actually trying to push the thing to jump start it! We all had an adventure that day. Lesson learned, though: Meridith and I use the parking deck now whenever we're downtown.

The Case of the Stolen Dress

"Hello, and thanks for calling Walters & Walters. We're on a shoot right now, but leave a message and we'll return your call soon."

Beeep!

"Um, hi James, it's Cynthia. Hey, I wanted to call you because, well, my dress was stolen from the dress shop in Charlotte this past weekend. I'm in the car with my mom driving to a place in Winston-Salem and hoping that I can find something off the rack that will work for my wedding. I need to schedule another bridal portrait. I know the wedding's only two weeks away, but would it be possible to have another portrait in time to display at the reception?"

I hear that message and I'm thinking to myself, How in the world does a wedding dress get stolen? I could imagine the mugger in a dark alley: "Hand over your purse lady and nobody gets hurt. Oh, and that dress, is that a size four? Looks like my sister's size. Gimme that too!" Even by wedding-industry standards, this was one of the most bizarre things I had heard.

Once I caught up with Cynthia, she told me some of the story on the phone. I was surprised at how calm she was, until I realized that her mom probably had her on some mood softening prescription. I didn't get many details, but by the time I got home that night it was all over the news. Local news stations love a story like this, where they can use clichés about an evil business owner taking advantage of innocent people during one of the most special times of their lives. They dialed the drama way up showing interviews with several girls crying and drying their eyes with a tissue, being sure to use a camera angle that showcased the engagement ring. There was sad music and even the obligatory sound bite from the local sheriff saying, "We are determined to get to the bottom of this." It was an Emmy waiting to happen. The whole thing looked and sounded like a skit on *Saturday Night Live*.

It turned out that Cynthia's bridal shop was allegedly running a ponzi operation, taking payment in full for wedding dresses that were supposed to be delivered months later. The store used that money to order dresses that other customers had paid for months before. Even worse, they were also accused of buying used dresses back from brides who had been married for a while and selling them as brand new at full price. It wasn't just bridal gowns, though. If a bride got her dress there, it was a good bet that her bridesmaids' dresses were from there too. This was affecting a lot of people.

The news story alleged that the shop owner lost control of the scheme. From what people were telling me, prior to this incident, the store had a solid reputation as a high-end shop that carried the top designers. I guess the owner knew that she was in over her head and decided to make her mark in a dramatic way before going into hiding. She called several clients, told them the business was in trouble, and that the sheriff would most likely lock the place down in a few days. She also told them they would not be getting their dresses, for which they had already paid in full. Then in a total lapse of sanity, she dropped a hint that she would be leaving the store unlocked when she left that day, so that if they wanted to go by and get some things, no one would stop them.

As you might imagine, that news traveled fast, and soon it was bedlam. Crazed and angry brides converged on the shop and grabbed everything they could get their hands on. Of course, Cynthia didn't get that call. Her dress had already been delivered a few weeks before. We had even completed her bridal portrait just a week prior. The problem was that, after the portrait, Cynthia did what brides often do and returned her dress to the shop to be steamed before the wedding. It was hanging in the back room and was taken during the mad dash that stripped the store of nearly everything but the carpet.

I never heard how many people were involved in the looting, but by the time the police arrived to lock it down, most of the inventory was gone. Cynthia did find another dress, which I thought was even nicer than the first one. We completed portrait number two in time for display. Cynthia kept it all in perspective and ended up having a wonderful time on her wedding day.

I've been doing this long enough to know that I *haven't* seen it all. There is always something more sensational and even less believable around the corner waiting to catch me off guard.

Unwanted Attention

Walking around in public places while carrying a big camera makes people want to talk to you. When I lived in Greensboro, I loved scheduling photo shoots downtown. There are so many different looks to fit a multitude of photographic scenarios. In my own warped way, I thought of that part of town kind of like the venerable mullet hairstyle: it was all business in the front and a party in the back. If you're on Green Street, you'll see the granite and glass buildings you would expect to see downtown. Over the years, I shot a ton of model portfolios on that street because as a background, it gives the models a vibe that said, "Trust me, I'm a business professional."

Walk one block over on Elm Street, however, and you'll feel like you're in a totally different town. The only word to describe it is eclectic. With old-style storefronts, funky doorways, and local art, it's gritty, colorful, and nostalgic all at the same time. Between the two streets is the alley behind the Biltmore Hotel, which has always been a favorite location for its authentic urban decay look. For a visual artist, it's definitely the party in the back.

When I spoke to Kelly about her upcoming bridal portrait, she told me she wanted something different. No park or garden for her. She didn't want staircases, gazebos, fountains, or other random architecture that Southern women find attractive for reasons I still don't understand. Kelly wanted to go downtown and create bold, funky images unlike anything her friends would have. I love when clients say things like that. I always encourage people to do something in their personal style rather than what they think is expected or, even worse, what their friends did.

I met up with Kelly and her sister, and we began walking north on Elm Street. At that time, the downtown area was undergoing a massive revitalization to bring more people and business to the area. The advantage for me was that every time I visited, there were different things to see. It was never the same place twice.

We kept walking and as we found suitable locations or beautiful lighting, we stopped to do a few shots. Walking down the street with someone wearing a wedding dress gets people's attention. Most people give a brief double take. Older ladies and confident young ladies will tell the bride she looks beautiful or say "congratulations!" Then you have the random redneck who drives by in his muscle car, lays on the horn, and yells, "Woo! Get it girl!" I don't know what that means, but I'm sure it makes the bride self-conscious.

Walking down Elm Street, I noticed a red doorway just begging to be used in an image. I knew it was old because it was ornate with fantastic detail in the woodcarving. Not the kind of thing you could pick up at Home Depot. I loved the look of it and had Kelly stand with her back leaning against the cracked red frame. I positioned my light to create dramatic shadows and contrast. I also laid on the ground for a low and dramatic camera angle, one where the lines of the image would lead the viewer's eye from the detail at the bottom of her dress up to Kelly's face.

Accessory to Marriage

It took a bit of trial and error to get perfect balance of dramatic lighting and angle without looking like I tried too hard to do something cool. A few test shots into this setup I noticed a guy peeking his head out the door behind Kelly. I thought he would either try to exit the doorway or tell us to get lost. Instead, he motioned for me to come over and gave me his card. He explained that he had a photo studio upstairs and was selling everything in it. He went down a long list of the things he was getting rid of and said if I was interested to give him a call. While I was grateful for being given the opportunity to buy things from a stranger, daylight was fading and I was ready to get back to the shoot. We got our shot in the doorway and moved on.

About a block from the red doorway, we came to a small alley with some funky art sculptures. I thought it looked cool, but I wasn't sure how we would work Kelly into the scene. I have a real problem with photographers who try to be wild and crazy just for the sake of doing something different. You need the right combination of client, wardrobe, setting, lighting, and attitude to make any image believable. If any one of those elements are off balance, you look like you are either trying too hard or you make your client look silly and completely out of place. So about two shots into shooting in this alley, I realized it was a forced situation and it was time to go somewhere else. As I was suggesting this to Kelly a guy appeared from out on the sidewalk.

In a voice that sounded just like Chris Rock he said, "Hey, I noticed you're a photographer. I got this thing here I'm sellin'. If you want it, I'll make you a good deal, just ten bucks."

"Wow, that is a great deal, I wish I had some cash with me," was my reply. That "thing" he was trying to sell me was a nice Italian-made tripod. I knew that it was worth way more than ten bucks because I owned one just like it. It would easily cost three hundred dollars new, so I felt pretty confident that it was stolen.

"Are you sure, man? I mean a deal like dis don't come along every day. I know you photographers need dis stuff and there's a cash machine around the corner. I'm making you a deal here."

We were all getting a little nervous and were ready to get out of there. The problem was, Mr. Deal-of-the-Day was standing between us and the only exit from the alley.

That's when Kelly glanced over with a look that said, "This guy's starting to freak me out. Get rid of him!"

After a few more rounds, I finally convinced the guy that even though I really appreciated his commitment to provide me with great photo equipment at incredible prices, I just wasn't in a position to purchase his obviously stolen tripod. The three of us were relieved when he finally gave up and moved down the street. We moved on to a spot where I used to like wrapping up an urban shoot. Despite the interruptions thus far, I thought it had been a very successful bridal session and I wanted to end it on a high note at the railroad tracks. This was back in 2002, before it was completely cliché to shoot a bridal portrait on railroad tracks. You couldn't pay me to do it now, but those were simpler times. The sun was getting low in the sky and glimmered beautifully down the tracks. Knowing that I wanted drama, I grabbed my custom infrared camera first and gave Kelly instructions to walk straight down the tracks for about fifty feet or so. Then turn around and walk back toward me.

The shot I had in mind was more about the place than the person. The element of infrared and the ethereal quality it brings create a dreamy yet grungy tension. Beautiful yet otherworldly, I dig that stuff. With Kelly barely four steps down the tracks, I began shooting test exposures and making adjustments to my composition. My intention was for her to turn around, walk toward me and I would begin shooting the "real" images.

Just as I was about to call out to Kelly to turn around a booming voice shouted from behind us. "I'll need you folks to come away from there. It's against the law to be on or near railroad tracks."

I turned around to see a police officer standing in the street behind us. I also saw that he had a familiar-looking tripod in his hand. I almost laughed, but I wasn't yet totally sure if we were in trouble.

Damn it, I thought to myself. Another five minutes and I would be in my car headed home. Now I've got to deal with this, and we're losing the sunset! I told the officer that I didn't know it was against the law; there were no signs around.

"It's a state law, they don't need signs, but I'll let you go this time. In most cases, I would need to issue a citation for trespassing. By the way, is this thing yours?"

"Not mine," I said, "but a guy just tried to sell it to me about twenty minutes ago."

"I saw the guy walking around with it. When I asked him about it, he threw it down and took off running. I chased him for a while but he got away. Could you give a description of him?"

"Yeah," I responded, "Remember Pookie from that movie *New Jack City*?" The officer chuckled to himself and nodded his head as he walked away. Some sessions seem to have the unintended effect of providing us with one distraction after another. While it's annoying at the time, it's fun to tell those stories years later.

Most Memorable Quotes Ever

"Sorry, I poot when I'm nervous."

A bride whispering to her wedding
planner, who was fluffing the dress
to send her down the aisle.
(The planner is still in therapy.)

Chapter 6
That's Just the Way It Is

Call it tradition, stereotyping, whatever you want, but there is a reason why some of the crazy wedding scenarios you've read about here show up in TV and movies. Some situations play out as reliably as the sunrise, others as unpredictable as the stock market. Having done this several hundred times has made me pretty good at knowing how people will behave in specific situations and predicting what will happen next.

Remember that opening scene in *The Wedding Crashers* movie when the two main characters are in the ceremony making a bet on which Bible verse would be read next? (Always put your money on 1 Corinthians 13—"Love is patient, love is kind…") Besides creating great images, half the fun of being at weddings is the bets Meridith and I make on things that are just as predictable, like which family member is most eligible to make a scene, or who will be the life of the party at the reception. We debate about who in the wedding party will hook up with each other, who is most likely to spend the rest of the evening in the bathroom, and if anyone is a favorite to be carried away in an ambulance.

We're wrong a lot, but we're right a lot too, and it's always fun when we call it. Because every wedding is like a theatrical production, we too become invested in the story and are drawn in by the characters' personalities and motivations. Their hopes, dreams, and future aspirations drive us to keep our eyes open as the story unfolds. Well, perhaps that's a little over the top, but we do enjoy the ~~freak show~~ people watching.

Going through life, I think people tend to take the things they are told and compare them to their own experiences in search of a general truth. Sometimes the two match, other times not. Either way, it's a life-long process that in most cases takes place on a subconscious level. It's our brain's way of taking what we know and organizing it into categories of what we expect of the people we meet and the places we go.

We call these generalizations stereotypes. As kids, we are told that generalizations strip away people's individuality of ethnicity, religion, or place of origin. Stereotypes assume that because one belongs to a certain group, others can predict how he or she will behave. Southerners speak slowly and marry their cousins; Catholics have lots of kids; whites can't dance; and so on.

As much as we would like to think that stereotypes are false, I have found that in certain situations, what I have heard to be true and what I experienced, have lined up more often than not. But I don't know of any fellow Southerners marrying a cousin (at least not a first cousin).

There are countless dynamics at weddings that I don't understand. Emotions can be mysterious and fickle. The minute you think you know what makes someone tick, their actions throw you for a loop. The second you think that because everything has gone well so far, it should continue to do so is usually when it all falls apart. We can try to plan for it, we can waste time asking ourselves why people act outrageously sometimes, or why unfortunate things happen during joyful occasions, but sometimes there is only one explanation. Sometimes, I find myself saying, "It is what it is."

Then I have to figure out how make it look good through my camera.

White People Dancing

About an hour after dinner, the toasts and the cake cutting are out of the way and the party is in full swing. Guests are on the dance floor getting their groove on and having a wonderful time. To the untrained eye, it simply looks like people celebrating and having fun. But I know there's more to it than that. As the person standing in the middle of the dance floor to document all this energy and merriment, I know that something miraculous is occurring. A magical transformation is happening within each and every person around me.

Doctors call it digestion, the process by which the body converts that nice meal they just ate into energy. This extraordinary process, coupled with the loud music, wild movements, and the sheer volume of people in the room gives way to a choice every person at the reception has to make: walk away from the party for a moment or just let one rip right there on the dance floor. No one would hear it over the music, and with so many other people around, it will be easy to feign shock for a few seconds to throw off any suspicion.

James D. Walters

My experience indicates, I am sad to say, that many guests prefer to stick with the party and choose the latter option. Of all of the wedding vendors, I think only photographers are remotely aware of this phenomenon. It's a point in the evening when the wedding planner is busy packing up the gifts, the DJ is stationed at his post, and the wait staff is cleaning the tables. But I am out among the guests in the middle of the dance floor walking through clouds of stench with my mouth closed trying to catch some great expressions as we all politely pretend that we didn't just smell that.

With all of that miraculousness happening, it's no wonder I capture so many people dancing with the oddest expressions. Can that be the only explanation though? After years of studying the subject, I feel I'm qualified to share my conclusion that white people really do make weird faces when they dance.

There I said it. No disrespect to my people, just an observation. Actually, white people don't dance so much as bounce around and point their fingers at the ceiling and each other. Like any group, a few have rhythm and are coordinated enough to make you proud. With most though, it's hard to tell if they're rocking out or if they forgot their seizure medication. Either way, those who are really getting their grove on have expressions that look either pained or angry or both.

You might be asking, "So, if white people make weird faces, what do other people do?" In my experience, they actually smile a lot. Their expressions mirror the energy of the music they are enjoying. They make eye contact with one another and show their excitement through the fluid movement of their bodies. This translates into a wide range of facial expressions representing all types of emotion, from simple joy to fiery seduction. It could be they're just not overthinking it.

Expressions are genre-dependent. For example, if the DJ throws down a hip-hop beat, you see people's eyebrows go down and their chins tuck in toward their chest. They look serious. Their lips go together really tight and poke out like they are trying to convince themselves they have soul and deserve to enjoy this song. For the guys, they just kind of stand there with that expression of anger and concern, moving their head from side to side, while the ladies are shaking their hips, throwing both hands up, elbows bent slightly, and whipping their heads from side to side. That's a move I call the pit sniff. At the point where the song gets good and a bridesmaid feels compelled to get down and smack the floor is also when two other ladies decide to grind on the nearest available guy.

On the other hand, if the band starts playing those God-forsaken Journey songs that every white person seems to love so much, you see completely different expressions. There's something about anthem rock that makes me want to shove ice picks in my ears. But most white people can't get enough. Unlike with hip-hop, their eyes close, their faces turn skyward, and their mouths open to a silent scream that looks like a cross between pain and yearning. For the ladies, one hand goes on their chest just under the neck and the head bobs up and down. As they lean back, their dominant hand goes up in the air with an open palm and elbows straight. For the guys, it's more of the same swaying back and forth with the exception that both hands can now point to the ceiling during the chorus.

There's no rump shaking to an anthem like "Living on a Prayer" or "Don't Stop Believing." But you'll see a lot of pointing at each other during the chorus as if to say, "Hell yeah, man! I totally identify with the message in this song. I believe in Tommy and Gina and, damn it, as long as I live, I'll never stop believing. Never!"

I capture weird expressions on the dance floor because, whether they want to admit it or not, people don't know the real words to half of these songs. But who's going to hear them slaughter it out there? They sing their hearts out with a healthy dose of "la la, ummmhmmm!" to fill in the parts they don't know. Thank God I'm only getting the visual on that.

The most entertaining thing to watch is when the skinny white girls go berserk acting out a song that was obviously not written to describe skinny white girls. Let the DJ throw out some "Brick House" or "Baby Got Back" and the whole place goes nutty! The guys are into it because they're looking at their girl thinking, Yeah, wouldn't that be nice. And since every skinny white girl thinks her butt is big anyway, this gives her four minutes to feel great about it. I can always count on lively expressions during "Baby Got Back" in the verse right after "Fonda ain't got a motor in the back of her Honda." It only happens 99.99 percent of the time. All the girls point aggressively at the guys and scream, "My anaconda don't want none, unless you got buns, hon!" Those are priceless memories right there.

Most Memorable Quotes Ever

"Tonight's gonna be awesome! I bet she's a screamer!"

Spoken by a drunk groom to the bride's mom as the couple made their final exit.

He Doesn't Love You Like That

E very few years, we encounter a couple that leaves us scratching
our heads. I'll be at the wedding, looking at Meridith saying,
"Seriously? How the hell did this happen? Does no one else see
what I'm seeing here?"

Phillip and Monica were a great example of a couple who had
no idea that they loved each other for very different reasons. I had
not met Phillip before the wedding day, but he seemed to have a
lot going for him. He was handsome and projected a warm, engag-
ing personality. I could only guess that he was successful at his job
because the clothes and car were all very nice. He was excited to be
getting married and really liked to have his picture taken. A lot. I
took photo after photo of him doing this or that, standing this way,
standing that way. All at his suggestion, mind you.

At that time I was training an assistant named Katherine. She
worked with me that day as I photographed the guys before the ceremony. After we wrapped up and were walking to the next building
to see the ladies, she asked, "Did he seem a bit, well, effeminate to
you?"

When I look through my camera, I tend to get into a zone and
there are certain things I just don't notice. Things like traffic that

might run me down, or the fact that I may be ruining my suit by rolling on the ground to get the best angle. I'm there to create stunning images.

I told Katherine, "I mean sure, his nails were impeccable, but I didn't notice a lisp or hear him humming any Streisand tunes. And the groomsmen, they didn't break out into any Broadway dance numbers, or exhibit any other cliché gayness."

Katherine laughed, "No, I'm serious."

"Nah, I didn't really notice."

After the ceremony, I photographed Phillip and Monica together. It was then I noticed major red flags. I can tell a great deal by how a man interacts with his new wife. True personalities reveal themselves in subtle ways. The range goes from childish and insecure to loving and reverent. It can have a lot to do with the age of the couple or if one of them has been married before. It's important never to judge something or someone based upon what your eyes see. You have to go into the deeper motivations that are driving those actions to get the complete story.

Phillip adored Monica. It was obvious by the way he looked at her that he was smitten, which on the surface is a positive thing. As time passed, it became clear that his feelings toward her were a little different than we are used to seeing. He would hold her close and constantly adjust her hair or veil. Most women I've met would have smacked him for touching the hair, but Monica didn't seem to mind. At one point, he even suggested specific makeup adjustments she could make to "freshen up her look" for post ceremony photos. His world revolved around her, and once the ceremony was over and they were together, it seemed like she was the only thing he could focus on.

I began to recognize that he was treating her the same way that a little girl treats her favorite baby doll. Holding her tight, fussing over her hair and clothing, and making sure that her every need was met. Phillip constantly adjusted her dress and kept her right by his side all day long. Most women I know would have flipped out after about ten minutes of such intense interest in their appearance, but Monica seemed to love the attention she received from Phillip. I'm sure she took his affection at face value and thought she had caught herself the perfect man. If anyone in the family or wedding party had any concerns, they certainly didn't show them that day.

As Meridith and I drove home from the wedding, I had so many unanswered questions.

"What just happened back there?" I asked her.

"What do you mean?"

"You didn't get the vibe that Phillip might not have married the right girl, or that maybe he shouldn't have even married a girl?"

"Just because a guy has freshly buffed nails and is really into the way his girl looks is no reason to put a rainbow sticker on his car."

"Yeah, I get that. But still, I think we just took pictures of a guy who might not know he's gay, marrying a straight girl who definitely has no idea he's gay."

"I don't know if you're the best one to judge. You were twenty years old before you realized the Bee Gees weren't girls. They all married women."

"Exactly, so did this guy! Look, I'm not saying that there's anything wrong with being gay, unless you go out and try to marry someone of the opposite sex. That's just weird."

"They're both pretty young. Who knows? They were awkward, but seemed to be into each other."

As we do a few weeks after each wedding, we delivered the photos. Monica sent me a note expressing how much they loved them and they were excited to begin working on the album. Almost a year passed between the wedding day and when we finally heard back from Monica about finalizing the wedding album. It was an uncomfortable conversation, and it was obvious she had been working up the courage to call and had rehearsed what she was going to say. She told me that she and Phillip parted ways some months ago after realizing that they were better as friends than they were as husband and wife. She didn't get into too many details but did tell me that Phillip had recently moved in with his friend Stephen and that even though things didn't work out, she was still interested in having a wedding album. She explained it in a way that offered no real information, but made it easy to read between the lines.

At least they discovered their issue within a few months. Sometimes people get so hyped up about getting married that they see the wedding as the destination rather than the starting point that it truly is.

Give the Guy a Break

Expectations are a funny thing. When you anticipate any situation in life, it's normal to have at least some idea about how you would like it to happen. Some brides have more specific ideas about their weddings than others, and a special few have the ability to successfully communicate that vision to those around them.

If there is one photograph that I have received the most requests for over my career, it is from brides asking me to capture the expression on her groom's face as she begins her walk down the aisle toward him. It's a magical moment. Hearing the music thunder to a deafening and joyous crescendo, she realizes her wait is over. A last fluff of the dress and both sanctuary doors swing open in front of her. She locks eyes with her true love and takes that first step toward her destiny.

Her groom is at the far end of the aisle staring in dumbfounded amazement at her radiance. Just a few more steps and they can be together forever. He is so smitten by her beauty that he has the brightest smile imaginable plastered across his face. Or perhaps it's a tearful expression showing that he is overcome with a flood of emotions for the entire time she walks toward him. Her field of view narrows, the crowd around them melts away, and he is all she can see.

All the while, I train my lens on his expressions of adoration and take a few dozen pictures to document every nuance. In the years ahead, she will revisit those photos that so clearly portray his devotion to her and know beyond any doubt that she is truly loved.

Well ladies, I have to admit, that certainly does sound magical. It's just a shame that it rarely happens that way. Expectations are one thing, but reality is a whole different ball of wax. While I'm sure he loves you and all, unless he knew in advance to do that stuff you are envisioning, he probably won't.

I learned this the very first time a bride insisted that she "had to have that shot, you know the one where he's gazing at me as I walk down the aisle."

Chris and Toni were all set to marry on the terrace of a gorgeous historic mansion in view of a mountaintop in Blowing Rock, North Carolina. The location overlooked the valley, and we hit the jackpot on timing because as far as you could see into the distance, the world looked like a patchwork quilt of rich fall colors. Red, yellow, and orange textures blended into a breathtaking landscape.

The week before, when I spoke with Toni about wedding-day details, she emphasized that her only photo request was to have a picture of Chris's expression as he watched her walk down the aisle. I knew this going into the day and had already visited the location to see the set up and how long the aisle would be. The longer the aisle, the more chances I get to work between his blinking. I was all set and felt confident that I could make this happen for her. This was nothing new, of course. I had created this very type of image for dozens of other couples. But I had never had a client place so much emphasis on it until I worked with Toni.

A great deal of time, thought, and effort go into a bride's decisions regarding how she'll look on her wedding day. Her dress and veil are the obvious elements, but then there are the makeup and hair trials, multiple dress fittings, alterations, and myriad other details from which the groom is happily insulated. I can see where a bride might think, I want a photo to remember his face when I start walking down the aisle and he sees this all put together. He's gonna loose his mind!

When the time came for the ceremony, I was in the ideal position to make Toni's vision of capturing the perfect look from Chris a reality. She appeared with her father from outside the courtyard, just beyond the view of the guests. The string trio changed songs and the minister motioned for the guests to stand. Toni rounded the corner looking fabulous, and I knew the moment had come.

There was a window of about twenty seconds to get this shot so I focused on Chris, composed the scene in camera, and took the first few shots while waiting for Toni to walk a little farther so she would be in the frame.

To tell this story properly in a still photograph, it's important to avoid simply filling the frame with his face alone. The story here is not really about him, it's about him adoring her. So Toni needed to be part of the image to give the scene context. The sunlight was hitting her veil beautifully and after a few more seconds ticked by, her shoulder appeared in the frame.

I really started shooting then. Not obnoxious motor drive style, but a decidedly aggressive "we gonna make this thang happen" pace with the shutter. Behind the camera my excitement grew as all of the elements of the perfect shot fell into place.

I'm thinking, This is it! The light, the girl, the magic... Oh wait. Where's the magic? Why is he looking at her like that? Why the hell isn't he smiling? *Dude, you look like you just smelled something foul!*

The pressure inside my head grew unbearable as I mentally screamed at Chris. I remembered all of the thought and discussion that had been put into this moment turning out perfect. Now his stupid, expressionless face was ruining it.

For God's sake, just one smile, a smirk, anything! Come on man, you're killing me! This is almost over!

Chris just stood there stone-faced, motionless, with a stare that led you to believe that his mind was far away. Toni reached the altar and the moment was over.

There was nothing more that could be done. As Toni reached Chris, he acknowledged her by pressing his lips together in that expression that guys use to greet other guys they don't really know. The one that's paired with a nod of the head as if to say, "I acknowledge you, but since I don't know you, I am not going to seem friendly or approachable." He then turned around and the ceremony began.

I was so mad I wanted to kick something. As I stood there in that beautiful place reeling from the opportunity that had just been ripped away from Toni and me by that emotionless robot of a man, it occurred to me that no one ever let Chris in on the plan. Mostly, I was mad at myself for falling into the trap of creating unrealistic expectations for a situation I had no control over. Chris had no idea that he was supposed to look at her a certain way. Guys don't really react to the drama of a big reveal the way women think they should. There were a thousand thoughts running through his mind in the half a minute it took her to get to him, and the poor guy was just trying to keep it all together.

Magic does happen. As I said, I have captured that very image many times before and since Chris and Toni's wedding. When it happens the right way, it is magical. The important thing to know about magic is that it works on its own time. You can't plan for it. You can't put it on a shot list or a schedule. If you do, then it's just a recipe for disappointment.

Most Memorable Quotes Ever

"That was the most awkward three minutes of my life."

Said by the bride to the groom following their first dance.

Falling Out

You only have to watch one episode of that show with the funny home movies to see a half-dozen or more clips of people standing up at the altar during weddings and passing out. You're probably watching and thinking to yourself, Does that really happen? Let me assure you that it does. Summers get hot in the South, and sometimes a little heat mixed with a little stupid can equal a stellar demonstration of gravity as a major force in the universe that is not to be challenged.

Sometimes it's the groom, but more often it's a groomsman who was too busy telling old college stories about sneaking into the Tri Delta house when he was supposed to be listening to the church lady reminding them not to lock their knees while standing up at the altar.

My guess is the last thing that crosses his mind is beer, bad idea. Boom! Next thing he knows, two groomsmen are on either arm escorting him to the front row next to where his buddy's mother is sitting. All eyes are on him, and he wishes he could melt into the seat cushion and disappear.

It's one thing to see a delicate four-foot-seven-inch tall, ninety-eight pound bridesmaid go down in the middle of a ceremony.

You almost expect it. But when 260-pound Jethro goes down during the ring exchange, well that's just embarrassing. It happens usually in the heat of summer in a country church, where little old ladies are using the programs to fan themselves and the floors are made of hardwood that's going to leave a mark when someone's head hits it.

The most people we have seen go down in one year was four, all at weddings in May of 2006. We called it the year of the crash. The first one occurred at Lilly and Chad's wedding in Charlotte. Lilly was surrounded by an enthusiastic group of four ladies and Meridith, and I had a lot of fun photographing them about an hour before the ceremony. We were locked away with them in the bride's parlor as they waited out the last twenty minutes before the service. As often happens, someone magically produced a bottle of champagne and five cups for a festive toast. The bubbly was poured, and the girls instinctively gathered into a circle and held their glasses in the middle. Words were said, laughs were had, and, before we knew it, the champagne was gone.

That didn't seem to be a problem at the time. The ceremony music began and Lilly and her bridesmaids took their place at the back of the church. If you remember my description of the "standard format," this wedding was exactly that: twenty minutes of formalities then off to the party. That was the plan anyway. The couple exchanged vows halfway through the proceedings.

"I Chad, take you Lilly to be my…" THUD! The sound was loud, but since my camera was focused in close on Lilly's face at the time, I didn't see what happened. I lowered the camera from my face, and no one seemed to be moving. Chad and Lilly were still facing each other and holding hands, though the rest of the wedding party was looking at the floor behind Lilly. The minister motioned for the couple to continue.

"…lawfully wedded wife, to love and to cherish, and forsaking all others until we are parted by death."

When Chad finished his line, the minister knelt down to attend to the bridesmaid who I just realized was missing from the lineup. Whoa, someone did go down! I thought. I was in the back of the church and couldn't see that the second bridesmaid from the left had fainted. No one caught her; no one rushed in to help her. Everyone just stood frozen letting her lie there until the vows were spoken. I guess vows are a big deal, huh?

"Luckily, besides being a Minister, I am also a paramedic." He told the crowd. "This young lady will be fine. We'll let her have a seat and then finish getting these two married."

It turned out that the glass of champagne just before the wedding was more than Lilly's friend could handle and made her head spin by the time the ceremony began. Ten minutes in and she just couldn't hold it together for the rest of the ceremony.

The other three crashes we witnessed that month were similar only in the sense that they all occurred during the ceremony. Strangely, none were alcohol-related. One was heat stroke at an outdoor ceremony. Another was a huge groomsman who made the mistake of locking his knees for too long. It took several guys to get him off the floor, and he sat in the front row feeling like an idiot for the rest of the service. The final one was a bridesmaid who forgot to eat or drink anything that day. Her neglect caught up with her, and she began to sway before her legs gave out during a piano solo. She is the only one of the three who was caught before they hit the ground.

Passing out during the wedding from counterintuitive behavior is bad enough. Missing your friend's wedding because you did something stupid the night before is worse. I walked into one groom's suite about an hour before his ceremony. Shawn and all of his groomsmen except for one had nearly finished dressing. I thought it was really odd to see one guy still in the bed with the covers pulled up around him sleeping while eight other guys were buzzing around him in the same room. I figured that maybe he was not a groomsman and didn't need to get ready until later. Then I learned that Pete was indeed a groomsman. According to what was already a legend, Pete got really hammered the night before and fell off the roof of a car. Like you, I also wondered how he ended up on the roof of a car, but I'm not one to ask a lot of questions, so we'll never know that part. They finally did get him to dress and meet us down stairs for just a few pre-ceremony photos.

Two shots into photographing the group of guys, Pete grabbed his head and slumped over. He didn't fall, but was assisted by two guys to the other side of the room to sit down. All attention shifted from the photos that had to wrap up in five minutes to the sick guy's condition. A group of at least a dozen concerned people surrounded him.

Some knew him and wanted to help; others didn't know him but wanted to be in the middle of the situation. The bride's sister-in-law, Karen, began asking him several questions. Then another lady who I could tell liked to worry herself with the problems of others began talking loudly about what everyone else should do.

"He doesn't look good. We should call a doctor or take him to the hospital, there could be something wrong with him."

All the while, Karen ignored the suggestion and kept talking to Pete, asking him questions about pain and if he could move his head in certain ways. As this was going on, Shawn the groom was circulating through the guests who were being seated for the ceremony. His wedding started in fifteen minutes and he had a plan.

As Shawn was outside working the crowd, not much changed inside the room except that the lady dropping comments became more vocal. "I just think we should call a doctor. It seems like the right thing to do to be on the safe side."

At that, Karen looked up at the lady and said as politely as she could, "I am a doctor, and from what I can tell here, it looks like he has a concussion. If you wouldn't mind being the one to call the hospital, to let them know he is on the way, that would be great."

About that time, Shawn appeared with a guest who had just been seated for the ceremony. "Hey guys, this is my cousin Chelsea's fiancé, Nolan. He wears the same size jacket and pants as Pete, so if we can get them into the bathroom to change, we'll still be able to walk down with eight guys."

As the grandparents were being seated, the men quickly switched clothes and Pete was shipped off to the hospital. Eight groomsmen emerged and the ceremony happened as intended. None of the guests had any idea that there was a stunt double in the group. Stand-in groomsman number 6 did a flawless job and really got into his role of helping balance out the symmetry of the wedding party. He was also a pro at that thing groomsmen do: stand in one spot and look on as the happy couple is married.

All That for Nothing

The decoration and details that are either addressed or ignored at a wedding can tell me a lot about the family who's throwing the party. If the bride is creative, formal, completely boring, or if she could just not care less about any of it, the clues are all right there. Sometimes a glance or two lets me know that this is really more the mother's wedding than the bride's.

It's not about the amount of money spent, either. Meridith and I have seen fantastic weddings put together on modest budgets because the bride and her family put their hearts, souls, and all their creativity into the visual details. We had so much to work with and could hear the guests all day commenting on how wonderful everything looked.

On the flip side, we have attended more events than I care to count where an ungodly amount of money was spent, but just one look around let us know that these people had no heart or soul for their wedding. We knew that while they considered it to be an important day for their family, it was obvious that they were afraid to stray from what their friends might consider to be socially acceptable. This fear can lead to a situation where people just do whatever their friends did regarding visual details like flowers, programs, and reception decor. The result is a beautiful event that looks a lot like the last beautiful event we photographed. Just change the names, the faces, and carry on.

I guess I should have known what I was getting into when I walked into the venue on Peyton's wedding day and saw that not only was everything the pinkest Pepto-Bismol color scheme I'd ever seen, but it was also Barbie themed.

Oh joy, I thought to myself. This reminds me of my three-year-old daughter's room. Looks like we have ourselves another princess.

As far as creativity and bringing a theme to life are concerned, it can really help to have a good wedding planner, and Peyton had one of the best. Being familiar with her work and high-level of taste and class, I could only imagine how their design concept conversation began.

> **Planner:** "So Peyton, do you have any favorite colors or themes that you would like to incorporate into your wedding?"
>
> **Peyton:** "Well, I like pink, which I think would work well for the spring time. What do you mean about a theme?"
>
> **Planner:** "You know, sometimes people want to highlight the things that brought them together and make that a theme. Like the school where you met, or places you've traveled together, or an interest or activity you both have in common."
>
> **Peyton:** (twisting her golden locks of hair) "Well, people always say we're like Ken and Barbie, and I really like Barbie. Could we do that?"

Planner: (sitting a bit stiffer in her chair now)"Umm, ehh, hmm, well, I suppose we can do anything. Are you sure?"

Peyton: "Yeah, that's a great idea, let's do it. Design us a Barbie and Ken wedding!"

This was one of those weddings that all of the vendors involved had been anticipating for the entire year. No expense was spared, which always gets vendors excited because they know they can go all out and show their talents on a grand scale. I heard time and again that the budget had no ceiling, and Peyton's dad said he wanted the very best for his only daughter. He had himself a "Daddy's girl," and Peyton played him like a master violinist. He made sure that anything she wanted would happen. It turned out that she had expensive tastes and wanted quite a lot.

Weddings on that scale are fun and challenging for us because all of the vendors involved—from flowers and cake to venue and invitations—are so excited to show off their work that they unconsciously pressure us to make sure the wedding ends up as a feature in a magazine. We have to strike a balance between keeping our industry friends happy and getting our primary work done for the family who has commissioned us.

The majority of wedding vendors I have worked with over the years have conducted themselves as professionals. Contrary to what a few might imagine, we don't sit around comparing clients' budgets. But I did hear through the grapevine that Peyton's floral budget alone could buy you a small house, and the cake cost roughly the same as my first car. The dress itself cost in the low five-figure range, but I heard that from Peyton's mom. It was truly a sight to behold. Straight from the designer's showroom in New York, it was bejeweled, bedazzled, and without a doubt the most sparklelicious thing I had ever seen. Not only that, but it was super low cut. I remember reading somewhere that if Barbie were a real person, her bust size would be somewhere around a 42 double D. Peyton wasn't too far off that mark. She was a curvy, rather busty girl herself, and the way the top of her dress plunged was enough to make any straight man with a pulse do a double take.

The stage was set for an ideal Barbie and Ken scenario. However, David, the groom, reminded me less of the clean cut and strong-featured Ken and more of a member of a teen boy band. He had fancy boy earrings and, well, even though all of my Barbie and Ken knowledge is derived from the *Toy Story* movies, I'm pretty sure that Ken never had earrings. David was nice enough and, even though we had never met before, he seemed to enjoy the process of making photographs and was an all around good sport.

Peyton, on the other hand, was coming to the realization that she bought a dress she loved to look at, but was a pain to wear. It was fitting tight in the bodice, which doesn't do a thing to help you catch a breath. She complained that it was super heavy and not easy to move around. It's funny how some women don't imagine themselves actually having to walk or sit or move when they're standing in front of a mirror and falling in love with a dress at the bridal salon. So between the imagined heat, the shortness of breath, and the weight of all of those thousands of crystals, we weren't getting a great deal accomplished with the ladies' photos. But what we were able to do looked fantastic and oh so sparkly.

Much to Meridith's and my collective happiness, the whole Barbie portion of the theme was played down in most areas of the venue. A few references here and there, but you had to be looking for it, almost like an inside joke that only close friends and good observers would notice. I thought to myself, it's a damn good planner who can take a cheesy theme and make it obvious only to the people who are looking for it.

It was still pink as hell though. Not just one shade of pink, it was all of them, pastels, hot pink, and every imaginable shade between.

When the reception began, Peyton changed into dress number two, which was a light and comfortable option for the throw down that ensued when our friend DJ Randy B. got things fired up. The reception adhered closely to the standard format. Drunk, white people trying their best to dance but in reality only making angry faces at each other, pointing in the air, and flailing all over the place. The young chicks were grinding on their dates and the older folks were shagging to the same song as if it were beach music (which it was not). It's like two different parties were going on the same dance floor.

By the end of the evening, Peyton and David had enjoyed a true fairy tale of a day. They happily exited through the crowd and jumped into the brand new Lexus that was their final wedding gift of the night. Even though Peyton's father would never again see those few hundred thousand dollars he spent on that one day, he appeared to have a great time and felt satisfied that he had made his little girl happy.

A few weeks after their wedding, I had all of the images edited and was really happy with the results. As we normally do, we sent the couple their package of photo goodies and waited anxiously to hear screams of joy in the form of a phone call or email. We waited a month and heard exactly nothing. I followed up with voicemails and an email or two with still no response. Creative people are well known as being overly needy of feedback regarding their work. Do you love it? Hate it? Either way is fine, but we want to hear something. Silence drives us crazy because the most demotivating thing is to pour our hearts and souls into a project that no one cares about.

People get busy, we were busy too, so we moved on and figured they would get in touch when they were ready to approve the album. A few months passed when one day I was in my car driving back from a lunch meeting and looked down to see that I'd missed a call from an out-of-town number I didn't recognize. There was a new voicemail:

"Hello Mr. Walters, this is Detective Tomlinson from the Salisbury Police Department. I'm calling in reference to some photography work that you did for a family here by the name of Copeland (not their real name). We are conducting an investigation related to this family and the wedding and will need for you to confirm information related to the services you provided to them."

This was a first. I immediately called the planner I worked with on their wedding to see if she had received any similar calls or could tell me what was going on. Did something bad happen that night after the wedding and they need our pictures for evidence? Is whatever this investigation about the reason that we had heard absolutely nothing at all from Peyton or David since the wedding? Crap, did somebody die?

My mind was racing, but my call to the planner went straight to voicemail. I tried my best to leave a message that was pleasantly vague. "Hey Donna, James here. I just got a call from someone regarding the Copeland wedding and was wondering if you have received any calls yourself? Thanks!"

A few hours passed before Donna called back and told me that she had received a call from the detective a few weeks before. He explained that Peyton's dad was being investigated for allegedly embezzling several hundred thousand dollars from his partners in their real estate company. It was a number that was roughly equal to the total of the wedding with a little left over. The detective wanted all of the vendors' contracts, payment dates, and receipts so that they could build evidence that showed a pattern of money going out of the company to cover wedding expenses. Donna said that she was stunned when she found out. But it did answer a lot of questions she had kept to herself along the way, like why were the checks for her services and many of the other vendors coming from people other than Peyton's father? Why did he call two weeks before the wedding and ask if it was possible to cut the flower budget in half?

Apparently, the investigation had been in progress well before the wedding. I know that we booked that wedding over a year before it happened, so there was plenty of time for things to build. We turned over our records and payment history and never heard from the detective again.

We also never heard back from Peyton or David, and I found out why during an industry-networking event. It had been more than eighteen months and I happened to run into one of Peyton's college friends who attended the wedding. It took us a second to realize how we knew each other, but as soon as we did I told her that the next time she saw Peyton, please tell her that I would love to wrap up their album and get it to them. She gave me that look of minor pain mixed with embarrassment that said, "Prolly not gonna happen." She told me that they were not likely to last much longer as a couple, and I shouldn't be surprised if I never hear anything from them.

All that planning, all of those flowers, that dress, our beautiful images, her dad faces a long trial and perhaps jail time—and for what? It's certainly not the first time that one of our couples didn't make it very long, but considering that the planning lasted longer than the marriage, I have to shake my head in bewilderment over the whole thing. Sometimes people are so caught up in the excitement of planning their wedding that they create a fantasy world where anything is possible and nothing can go wrong. Those are often the ones who forget about going back to reality afterward, and sometimes things don't end the way they imagined.

Estate Planning

There's a phenomenon among Southern mothers of the bride (MOBs) who are very deliberate when ordering pictures of their daughters to display in their house. It took a few meetings with different families before I learned to factor in the eventual death of the bride's parents into their portrait order.

You just read that and thought, it's getting near the end of the book, and now he's just making stuff up. Not so. When discussing portrait options with many a bride and her mother, the banter is fairly consistent:

> **MOB:** I really like that one on the top left. What do you think?
>
> **Bride:** I don't love that one. It just seems like I'm looking right back at myself.
>
> **MOB:** That's what I like about it. I like to see you smiling back at me.
>
> **Bride:** I mean, I don't hate it. It's just not my favorite. If you like it though, go ahead and get it. It will be hanging in your house so I'll only see it at the holidays.

> **MOB:** Well yes, but I want to make sure we get
> one that you like too, because when I die it will end
> up in your house.

The expression I see next lets me know that last comment whipped up a flurry of thoughts in the bride's mind. She's saying to herself: "I get that when she dies? Why are we talking about dying right now? I might force myself to like that pose, but I'll never like the gold frame she'll put it in. I guess I can change that, but I'll be dealing with all of her other stuff too, like that enormous china cabinet and her collection of Precious Moments figurines. Now I'm overwhelmed."

We're careful to choose the perfect pose so that the bride will one day, hopefully far into the future, be happy to inherit the portrait. But if there is a sister who has been married already, it brings a new list of considerations and anxiety for the MOB. This new portrait needs to be as good but not better than the first daughter's. They usually want it photographed in a similar style, so if older daughter used a super traditional photographer who created her portrait in a studio on the black background with a wicker bench and a fern slightly behind the bride (as if those things even go together), then I get the fun experience of having a somewhat uncomfortable conversation about how "Jimmy don't do that!"

It usually ends with a compromise and me reminding everyone that one daughter's style may be different from the other's, and they want to be sure that is reflected in the portrait. You can be certain though, that whatever we end up producing will be printed the same size as the first daughter's and displayed in an ornate gold frame that everyone over fifty thinks is so awesome.

I'm looking forward to finding out if I start loving gold frames when I reach my fiftieth birthday. We shall see.

Most Memorable Quotes Ever

"You put a dollar in the hat, down a shot, and dance with the bride. Welcome to Pittsburgh!"

DJ explaining the dollar dance to this Southern boy.

Chapter 7
A Glimpse Into My World

By now you're thinking that I've either got the coolest job on the planet or the lamest. Get paid to show up at a party, watch the people get wild, and take a few pictures of it all. Sometimes I wish it were that simple and superficial. Here's the thing: my clients hire me to do something very important for them. They want me stop time and help them live forever.

It sounds dramatic, but even with all the technology available, a well-executed photograph or video is often the closest thing to a time machine that we can experience. Your daughter might be all grown up, but in that photograph on your wall, she's still four years old, and just looking at it helps you recall her mischievous laugh. Your grandparents have passed on, but a quick study of the five or so photos taken at their wedding and you feel an appreciation for the life they lived, the legacy they created, and a stronger sense of connection to them.

Because we document personal history for families, we take what we do seriously. For most people, it's really easy to put off having professional photographs made of themselves or their loved ones. They want to wait until they're thinner, less busy, or when the kids' front teeth are finally in. Whatever the reason, it makes sense for them to wait for a special occasion like a wedding to come along and force them into it. When a loved one dies, photographs become prized treasures, especially if the last few depicted good memories. The realization hits that there will be no opportunities to make more.

James D. Walters

Photography is an endeavor that countless people have an interest in and many take up as a hobby. Some make it a career, while others go far beyond that to become completely consumed by it. It's a craft that can be studied and practiced for a lifetime without ever mastering all its aspects. While there is no shortage of misconceptions about photographers, especially wedding photographers, one commonality I have seen among the good ones is that they take the job seriously.

While there are fun times, big parties, and maybe a book's worth of stories after a decade or so, it's the touching stories that our clients share with us that make us continue giving our best. When we hear that a family who recently lost a loved one is comforted because of a photo we created for them, that makes us feel good. When a mom says that the image we made of her kid is the only one she has that shows his true expression, we get excited. One couple told us that a few years after their wedding they were having a rough time and near separation. They decided to get help, and their marriage counselor asked them to bring their wedding album to a session, point to each photo, and describe the feelings each were having in the moment the photograph was taken. That exercise helped them understand that they still cared for each other and their situation was fixable. We felt truly powerful after hearing their story.

Everything we do as photographers is about telling stories. The stories in this book are the funny ones, the outrageous ones. If you experienced one over the weekend, you'd say to your coworkers on Monday, "Oh my gosh, I have got to tell you what happened at my sorority sister's wedding on Saturday!"

It's fun to share those kinds of stories and see the reactions we get from others. But as photographers, we see everything. Not just the funny or the outrageous, we see the deeply personal and touching moments too. We witness far more moments that don't involve any drama or controversy but communicate true love and create a foundation for future generations of a family. Those are the kinds of stories that Meridith and I seek out with our lenses every week. Using our visual medium, we record the instant a story is created between two people, and we give them the ability to relive it many times through a photograph. In our view, that is an honor and a great responsibility. It's also a challenge, which is what keeps us on our toes and motivated to improve, even after all of these years.

Photographs themselves can be powerful. The most powerful ones tell stories that make the viewer want to know more about what he or she sees—who, what, when, and where. Photographs can bring back long-forgotten memories as much as they can inspire people to create new memories and do things they haven't yet experienced.

Good images move people. The crappy cell phone pictures we see so often on our social feeds might show you who or what was in front of the phone at the time. But even a crappy cell phone in the hands of a professional image-maker can allow them to convey more about the story than just who or what. The average person might look at the result and ask, "You did that with a phone?" The viewer will be gently reminded that it's not about the box that captured the light; it's the brain behind the box that makes the image look the way it does.

It seems as though everyone calls themselves a photographer today. No matter where you live, you can't walk outside and swing a dead cat without hitting a half-dozen faux-tographers. To all of you in my profession who respect the craft and work every day to move your art and vision forward, you have my sincerest admiration. To those of you who bought a camera and thought this would be a cool way to make money on weekends, well, bless your heart. I'll be praying for you.

The Serious Side of Celebration

When I began photographing weddings, it never occurred to me that I would receive so many calls each year from past clients requesting a photo to use at a parent's or grandparent's memorial service. It could be from a client I haven't heard from in eight or ten years, but when the need arises, they know how to get in touch, and a lot of them tell me the same thing. They say that the photo of their relative we made at the wedding was the last good one that wasn't "just a snapshot."

When I retrieve the requested image from our archives, I look at it knowing that person is now gone, and this photo is considered to be the last "good one" of them. That's when I have a little heart-to-heart with myself and ask, Did I do them justice in this photo? If I knew when I created this image that it would be this person's last proper portrait, would I have done this or something different? Those two questions drive the majority of creative decisions I make behind the camera and help me avoid anything that might be considered trendy or gimmicky.

James D. Walters

Over the years, I have gone into several sessions where I knew ahead of time that I would be creating the last official photographic record of that person. It's a heavy feeling to be charged with such a great sense of responsibility. During the session, I'll be looking through the camera, knowing that this person in front of me will be gone soon. I need to push my own feelings aside and keep the energy in the room positive so that the expressions I capture will be ones the family will want to remember. It's rewarding too because it forces me to do my very best work. In those cases, I know that the images I deliver will mean so much to the family for many years.

In most cases, I know what I'm getting into when there is a health concern with a portrait subject. I donate as much work as I can for a fantastic organization called Flashes of Hope. (flashesofhope.org). I know the steps necessary to emotionally prepare myself to walk into those situations. There have been times when I was blindsided mid-session with information that made me reevaluate my portrait strategy. As with so many things in life, those sessions start out like any other until someone drops a different paradigm on your head like one of those Looney Tunes anvils.

I learned an awful lot about the importance of doing my best while in the middle of a bridal session. We were about halfway through the different portrait setups. I was going about my business of fluffing Susan's dress, adjusting her veil, and tweaking my light for the perfect full-length image when her mother asked where she wanted

260

to go out to eat before heading to a charity event they were attending later that evening. I commented that it worked out well that Susan would be able to attend an event after having her makeup and hair professionally done.

"It's like getting two events for the price of one beauty appointment," I said.

That's when they told me that Susan was going that evening to donate her hair to a cancer charity, and in just a few hours her head would be completely shaved.

Inside my own completely shaved head, the record scratched for me in a big way. I suddenly felt heavy, and confused. First I thought, Damn it James, you've got to stop saying stupid shit like that. Then I began questioning if they were serious and, if they were, had I put everything I had into this session? Then I thought, But she gets married in four weeks, isn't she going to want some hair then? What am I missing?

They went on to explain that Susan was to begin chemotherapy the following week and would be losing her hair before the wedding anyway, so it made sense to donate it. This was the first I was hearing of any of this. I hope I maintained my composure on the surface, but inside my confidence evaporated for a few minutes. Even though I was still adjusting the dress and taking pictures as if everything was normal, in my mind I was screaming at myself, "Dude, this is for real! This better be the best work you've ever done. No do overs. Don't screw this up!"

Two weeks later, Susan and her mom came to view the portraits and choose their favorites. They were in good spirits, but quiet. Susan looked tired, and I could tell that treatment was taking its toll on both of them physically and emotionally. Bundle that with the excitement and stress of planning a wedding, and it was hard for me to imagine how they were getting along. I was nervous and hoped they would love the photos. We went through the images and they chose their favorites. I got to breathe a big sigh of relief and they had a great mother-daughter bonding experience.

I'll never forget the lesson I learned that afternoon: Every image we create is important and should mean something to someone. Since then, I take nothing for granted and go into each session asking myself, If this somehow ended up being the last image of this person, would I be proud to deliver it to their family?

Looking Good in Photos

Outstanding images of people looking comfortable and natural don't happen by accident. I could walk into a wedding with the biggest, baddest camera ever made, I could show up with all of my fabulous lighting and seven thousand years of experience, but if I don't communicate well with the people who are in front of the camera, the resulting images will look beautifully lit, well composed—and horribly uncomfortable.

On some photo sessions, I find myself being more of a body language coach than a photographer. Body language and expressions are a huge but overlooked part of photographing people. I have said it before and I'll never stop saying that subtlety is the backbone of sophistication. The nuance of body language in an image can tell the viewer volumes about the person in the photo. Most people only know how to, "Look at the camera and say cheese." What a waste that is. Facial muscles can convey so much more than a superficial "cheese." People are so conditioned to do this when a camera is pointed their way that there is little hope of rehabilitation.

Then there is the issue of wardrobe. It's unfortunate, but some folks just seem to choose clothing that fights with their body shape or size. Of course, everyone wants to look his or her best for photographs. That's part of the reason why they go to so much trouble to dress all fancy and put large amounts of product in their hair. Choosing the right outfit is a key source of stress for people who are getting ready for a photo session. Wedding couples have it a little easier because whether they look great or not, she's wearing a light colored dress, and he's probably wearing a suit of some kind. That greatly simplifies the wardrobe at least.

Most people are self-conscious enough with a camera pointing at them; add in a crowd looking at them, uncomfortable outfits, and a hectic schedule, and it's a wonder that we get anything done at all. There are however, a few things to keep in mind to be sure that you are looking good and feeling comfortable in front of the camera.

Ladies, Relax Those Shoulders

When being photographed, nearly every female does something I call the Hollywood shoulder. It's that move where she turns her body to the side away from the camera, turns her face toward the camera, and raises her shoulder until it nearly touches her chin. It must be genetic, and I would go as far as saying that 90 percent of the women I photograph do it. Even my two-year-old daughter did this when

I photographed her with a camera phone. No one taught her how, and she didn't see someone do it. It must be in the genetic code. Interestingly, guys never, ever do this. Ever.

Hollywood shoulder creates a few issues. First, the body language of having the shoulder up along with the rest of the body turned makes the subject seem either unapproachable or coy, depending on the facial expression. The second is that it covers a large part of the neck. That might not seem like a big deal, but visually, this move shortens the neckline and can make the person appear much thicker than in reality. Eliminating this problem is simple and it's the easiest ten pounds a girl can lose. Just relax, bring those shoulders down, and have a good time.

Guys, Put Your Hands on Your Woman

Guys are funny. There must be an unwritten rule somewhere that says if you are caught being affectionate then all of your college buddies will call you a fairy. Guys want to play it cool with their hands in their pockets, as if to say, "Yeah, I love you, I think you're great, but not really enough to show how I feel about you in front of other people."

My biggest pet peeve in wedding photography is when I see images of couples kissing each other and the groom's arm is dangling straight down by his side. Go ahead, look for them. They're on every website and in every magazine. I call it dead-arm love, when the groom's lips are saying, "I am so into you right now, I could sop you up with a biscuit," while his arms are saying, "Girls are gross, she's probably got cooties!"

All the man needs to do here is show a little interest by gently putting his hand on her waist and pulling her ever so slightly toward him. That's all. Simple, and I promise no one will make fun of him for doing it.

Ladies, You Don't Have To Smile In Every Photo

Seriously, sometimes it's okay to have an image that just looks like you when you're not high on life. Non-smiling images can be beautiful. Forcing a smile for the sake of a happy picture is a recipe for fake expressions and sore cheek muscles.

If your man makes your smile, that's great. If you're just a happy person then we love that too. But don't tell me that you think you look mad when you don't smile. You can look fantastic whether you smile or not, unless you start thinking about it too much.

Ladies, Sparkly Makeup Is Bad for Photos

It might look great when you're droppin' it low at the club, but clubs are dark and the eye shadow and powders that have shimmer in them will make you look like a clown once the light of day hits you in the face. People will see your pictures and wonder, "Why does she look like a surprised space alien?"

Guys, Lean toward Your Woman!

Similar to the ladies' phenomenon of the Hollywood shoulder, guys seem naturally inclined to maintain their personal space. When directed to get close, they habitually pull in close with their body and pull away with their face.

This leads to some interesting mixed signals from the perspective of body language. The resulting photo says, "My lower torso wants you madly, though the rest of me finds you to be hideous and repulsive." Leaning back like that can also create about four more chins that were probably not visible before. It's a hard truth that of all the things in life people want more of, chins never make the list.

So guys should remember to lean in. Not necessarily in a, "I want to lay you down by the fire," way, but rather to give off the vibe that he's slightly interested in her."

Ladies, Avoid Leaning Back

Similar to the shoulder suggestion, do everything in your power to avoid leaning back, whether it's away from your man or away from the camera. It puts your jawline closer to your neck and can easily add twenty pounds. I'm not talking about people who think they're overweight either; I'm talking about anybody with a chin and a neck, which includes most folks I've worked with.

It doesn't take much, but when you lean slightly forward, the skin under your chin either flattens out significantly or, depending on the camera angle, may not be seen at all. The jawline is better defined and if the photographer is worth a damn, they will be sure to create lighting that casts a slight shadow under the chin to further define and separate the jawline from the neck. This technique can easily take away ten to fifteen of those pounds I hear people complaining about.

How to Ruin Your Own Wedding

Weddings can be a lot like cars: they are both made of a multitude of moving parts that need to work together for a successful outcome. As with cars, most people are familiar with weddings but wouldn't know where to begin if they had to actually build one. Cars can also be expensive. Depending on your tastes and budget, you can spend anywhere from a few hundred bucks for an old beater on its last leg, to a few million on the latest Italian super car. Weddings are no different.

One of the biggest similarities that I have witnessed is that, just like with cars, it's easy for couples to wreck their own weddings. They don't mean to. They don't want to. It happens because they weren't paying attention to the signs or were distracted from what was most important at the time.

Since we're still milking the car analogy, have you ever driven around a crowded parking lot hoping a convenient space opens up? Just when you round the corner for the third time, you spot back up lights. You get excited and lock in on your destination. As the car backs up from a space that is right in front of the store, you think to yourself, Hallelujah, this is the world paying me back for all the good things I do! You put on your turn signal and your mind quickly goes into shopping mode. A few seconds pass before you realize that the person you thought was backing up had actually just pulled into the spot and then backed up just a little so they could park their car straighter in the space. You know how that infuriates you and makes you want to smack a bitch?

I do, because that's exactly how it feels when I get to a wedding that is beautiful and so full of potential only to discover that the couple is so distracted by scrutinizing every little detail that they are unable to enjoy any of it. They end up missing out on experiencing or even appreciating their day. I've seen brides fixate on minor variations in the colors of their flowers, scuffs on bridesmaid's shoes, or the way the reception napkins were folded. I've seen grooms spend their day obsessing over the schedule of events or whether his dad's new wife would try to pick a fight with his mom.

It's hard to watch. Part of me wants to scream at them, "Stop thinking! Just look around and enjoy this. It will all be over soon and tomorrow you will regret having spent one minute worrying about all of this stupid crap." But they can't help themselves. They have a disease that cannot be cured with screaming or reasoning. That's just how they are, and nothing I say is going to change it.

I do have a strategy with those people, though. It's a simple one that works with both toddlers and distracted perfectionists alike. I call it over-direction. There have been studies that concluded our brains are only capable of processing up to four thoughts at any one time. So if I give Mr. and Mrs. Type-A six different things to do all at once, suddenly the fact that their ring bearer's tuxedo jacket is a size too large tends to jump right out of their heads just long enough to get in a few decent photos.

My speech quickens as I tell them in rapid succession, "Both of you look over to your right, okay, now look at each other, pull in close, bring your hips closer too, okay, now bring your shoulders down, actually, let's just have her bring her shoulders down. Great, now look at the tree across the parking lot, now back at me, slight smile. Good! Now, facing each other, she'll bring her hands to his face and pull him in closer, okay. Done! Great job!"

It's incredibly exhausting, but overwhelming people who are preoccupied with worry is what you have to do sometimes to get the shot.

Another fantastic way to ruin your own wedding is to convince yourself that this day will be the most important, magical, and meaningful one of your entire life. A sure sign that you are on the road to success is if you find yourself having thoughts like this: It's *my* day. I'll take my time; they can't start without me. The weather will be perfect. Everyone in the family will get along, and when we are up at the altar expressing our undying love for one another, fuzzy baby bunnies will hop up from the meadow and lay dandelions at our feet.

This is good! It means the delusions are becoming hard-wired, and now the next step of spreading the word and convincing everyone around you to jump on your little crazy train should be a piece of cake. You go, girl!

Once you are sure that everything will go as flawlessly as imagined, start comparing your wedding day plans to what your friends did. This is essential and there are no shortcuts here. Maybe start by asking yourself a few of the following questions.

- Will it be nice enough?
- Will I have more guests than my brother and sister-in-law's wedding?
- What will my sorority sisters think?
- Will the ceremony appear to be more meaningful than my friend Suzanne's?
- Is judgmental Aunt Laverne going to be impressed?
- Will I look as good as my sister did in her dress, or should I get that gym membership now?

If you were a step ahead of me and already asked yourself a few of those questions, then congratulations! You are well on your way to wrecking that wedding in style. Just be aware, your insurance policy does not cover this type of damage.

It's also a good idea to be adamant that absolutely no one outside of your bridesmaids and mother should see you in your dress before the ceremony. By spending the first few hours of your day obsessing over who might be walking by outside as the parlor door is opened, and running to hide if anyone tries to say hello, you can successfully avoid any feelings of pre-ceremony nervousness. Of course, this behavior also limits most positive interactions with those around you, which destroys any hope of us getting decent candid expressions, but hey, a girl's got to choose her battles.

Finally, if you have all of the other pieces of the wedding-day-wrecking puzzle in place, but want to leave a lasting impression on everyone in attendance, the choice is clear: get loaded! I've found that brides and grooms who are too intoxicated or medicated to function, much less remember anything about their wedding day, are by far the ones who give their guests the most memorable experience.

I'm not talking about just few beers or glasses of wine to help loosen you up. That level of buzz can be a good thing for mellowing out type-A folks. I'm talking the freaky-nasty brand of stumbling, bumbling drunk that is guaranteed to get you a million views on YouTube. Oh, the fantastic stories they will tell around the water cooler on Monday after attending your reception, where you decided to climb up on stage with the band and perform mock fellatio with the microphone before ripping off your husband's shirt and sending him off to stage dive and crowd surf.

Whatever direction you decide to go in ruining your wedding, one thing holds true: you are in complete control of it. So go out there, give it your best, and make an impression that no one will ever forget. No matter how hard they might try.

My Advice

You may be wondering if I have any wisdom to share beyond a few cautionary tales regarding alcohol overindulgence. People often ask me: "Given all of the different things that you have seen over the years, what is the one piece of advice you would give a couple planning their wedding?"

No one poses the question quite that formally, but you get the idea. Wow, so many things come to mind. I would say to avoid giving anything flammable to drunk guests at the end of the night, but we've covered that a few times already. I could say that the spray tan you're thinking about will under no circumstances look how you imagined, but you'll do it anyway. I might be super annoying and insist that you must get your makeup done professionally or you'll look like a three year old who discovered their Mom's makeup drawer for the first time. But I'm going to go ahead and give you a little more credit than that. I could talk about the importance of staying hydrated on the wedding day, and how we've seen people pass out, but geesh, that's so boring. I'm going to get to the real stuff here, stuff you might not have read in the magazine checklists. If I were pressed to give a bride-to-be my most valuable insight it would be this:

Be yourself

It's your wedding. Wear the dress *you* like. Choose the colors *you* like. Wear the shoes *you* like (as long as they're not slippers or flip-flops, those are way lame). Don't let others' opinions drag you into something that doesn't reflect your personal style and tastes. Just because your parents went to their friend's daughter's wedding at the country club last month and now they have some "great ideas" does not mean that your wedding style has to be derailed. And even though your sister suckered you and all of her friends into wearing sea-foam green three years ago doesn't mean you have to abandon that Tiffany blue color scheme you've been dreaming about.

Let's all say it together. "It's my wedding!" There, didn't that feel great? So the next time your friend, the wedding planner wannabe, walks in with her fake bake tan, spike heels, and skirt hiked up her vag and tries to convince you that your wedding would "really be extraordinary if the guests were greeted by live tigers and elephants," you should have no guilt in calling BS on that and moving on with your day.

We live and work in the South and have seen our fair share of events where we walked away asking ourselves if that was the bride's wedding or her mother's wedding. Family pressures are real, and I get that. Traditionally, the bride's parents pay for the wedding, so in a way, it's their party, and their peers may judge them. But that doesn't mean you have to have silk flowers like they did it back in 1978!

With that said about personal style, I also understand that there are people roaming the earth who do not possess any style of their own. They are not sad, miserable, or even pitiful people, they are just busy, or distracted, or maybe just trying to wrap up business school at Duke and don't have time for all of this frou-frou wedding crap right now. That's okay; there is hope for those people too. It's called an experienced, professional wedding planner. Get one! Seriously, I'm not paid to say this, but a wedding planner is your best bet for creating the look and feel of your celebration in a way that doesn't stress you out. They are your organizer, decorator, enforcer, therapist, negotiator, and all around go between.

It's much easier for a planner to wrangle your wedding party or keep your other vendors in line. They don't just make everything pretty and tell you when to walk down the aisle. They make the tough decisions that often make the people around you nervous or mad. They deal with the rain plan. They tell your mom that silk flowers are not an option. They call a cab for your drunken cousin to get home from the reception and then decide what should be done with the girl who's passed out in the bathroom. Let them do the hard work. You will get the wedding you really want, and no one will hate you for it.

Now that I've gone on for several paragraphs about how this wedding is all about you. I'd also like to suggest that careful consideration should be made for your guests. You are inviting them to your party. You and your family are the hosts and you will be judged on how gracious you were and how comfortable you made their experience. So choose wisely.

I hear it from every client that guest lists can quickly get out of control. You started with a quaint venue and eighty people. By the time both sets of parents finish adding their friends, you find yourself trying to figure out how to pay for feeding three hundred and realize that you will need a bigger, more expensive venue. That's the time when you start researching how much money you could make if you sold your blood plasma every two weeks leading up to the wedding. Right after that, you'll begin daydreaming about running away and start another web search called "best places to elope."

Afterword

Every journey has an origin. The tricky part can be recognizing when a particular journey begins. Some are obvious. When you see two lines show up on a pregnancy test, you can be confident that an unforgettable journey has already begun. With other things though, a certain amount of stumbling around is involved until you wake up one day and realize that this life you live, this thing you do, is in fact your journey. Then you begin asking yourself, how did I get here? Sometimes only years of reflection can allow a person to revisit the point where everything changed for them.

I appreciate your willingness to travel back in time with me as I reflect on this aspect of my life's journey. The past dozen or so years have given me a better appreciation for what it means to be a part of so many people's personal histories, to share stories through images, and to hear how others have been positively impacted by them.

I encourage everyone I meet to decide for themselves what their story will be like. We often have little control over how our own stories begin or end, but we have a great deal of control over the paragraphs in the middle. So it's your move now. I'm finished writing and you're finished reading. It's time for each of us to go begin another journey worth talking about.

Author Biography

James Walters never imagined that he would photograph weddings. Early in his career as a commercial photographer, he perceived weddings as having too much emotional drama and not enough creative opportunities for photography. Fast forward fifteen years and hundreds of weddings later, it turns out that he was right about the emotional drama, but greatly enjoys the creative stimulation of working with interesting people and telling their stories through photographs. A resident of Raleigh, North Carolina, Walters works with his wife Meridith at their company, Photography by Walters & Walters. He also serves as a board member for the state chapter of the American Society of Media Photographers and the North Carolina Triangle chapter of the National Association of Catering and Events.